Andy
obscurit~~~ ~~~~~~~~~~ ~~~~~ ~~~
stand-up comedy career in 1997,
and, three gigs later, retired due
to popular demand. He came out of
retirement in 1999, since when he
has performed all over the British
Isles, as well as in America and
Australia.

Co-founder, -writer and -star of
the sporadically-acclaimed Radio
4 microsmashes 'The Department' and 'Political Animal', he
has also appeared on 'The Now Show', 'The News Quiz' and
'Armando Iannucci's Charm Offensive'. He has written for
several series of 'Bremner, Bird & Fortune' on Channel 4.

He is currently one half of TimesOnline's hit satirical podcast
'The Bugle', alongside John Oliver ('The Daily Show with Jon
Stewart'). One of iTunes' Podcasts Of The Year in 2007, 'The
Bugle' features Oliver and Zaltzman's trademark comedic
Molotov cocktail of incisive political comedy and outright
bullshit. He also writes for The Times newspaper.

Zaltzman's previous books include no previous books. He
lives somewhere in the United Kingdom, is currently married
to his first wife, and, at time of going to press, has very nearly
two children. He is completely unqualified to write a book on
economics. He prefers sport.

DOES ANYTHING eat BANKERS?

DOES ANYTHING EAT BANKERS?

ANDY ZALTZMAN

Old St PUBLISHING

First published in 2008 by Old Street Publishing Ltd
28-32 Bowling Green Lane, London EC1R 0BJ
www.oldstreetpublishing.co.uk

ISBN 978 1 905847 93 8

10 9 8 7 6 5 4 3 2 1

A CIP catalogue record for this title is available from the British Library.

Typeset by Old Street Publishing.
Printed and bound in Great Britain by Clays Ltd, St Ives plc.

For Vorax, The Tiddler and TBC

Foreword

by Sir Redvers Pook MBE,
former Chief Executive Officer of the failed
investment bank Woolf Gooch Proud

WELL, WELL, WELL. These are turbulent times for this old planet of ours: the economy was apparently sailing along calmly, until it transpired that the hull of the ship was made of salt. It duly dissolved, and the lifeboats were only large enough for a few big banks.

At Woolf Gooch Proud, we had front row seats as the whole financial disaster movie unfolded. The Vortex of Debt at the centre of the recent economic megastorm has been sucking down billions of dollars like a lonely vacuum cleaner guzzling a milkshake, and we paid the price when the Credit Crunch clamped its predictably spiky fangs so firmly and painfully around the world's economic nadgers. We had saddled ourselves with debt, and now debt was riding us like a birthday donkey. Our share price went downhill so fast that Swiss skiing fans were banging cowbells at it as it went past.

I and my colleagues tried everything in our power to reinflate the burst balloon of confidence in our firm. We put on serious faces, we sacked some of our nannies, we reduced our lunches to humble four-course snacks. We even took the trouble to spread the kind of rumours that in the past could be relied upon to ensure our share price would rise – we leaked a memo which told how our chief financial officer had just found a diamond tree in his garden that grows pure 24-carat jewels as big as a man's ventricle.

In the old days, this made-up plant would have been worth up to $10 billion of market capitalisation. But this was 2008, and these were more sceptical times, cynical times. People have had their fingers burnt – now they don't want to have those fingers buttered, popped in a bap, and gobbled.

Woolf Gooch Proud felt the economic pinch on our economic buttocks, and when we turned round to slap the perpetrator, we had cigar smoke blown in our eye by an ageing speculator saying "How about it then, sweetcheeks?" We hit the buffers. And the buffers hit us back, with a savage flurry of punches, and knocked us spark out.

I and my fellow directors lost almost everything in the space of a few months – pride, dignity,

respect, marbles, staff, and our favourite swivel chairs. We were left with nothing but feelings of guilt, and several million pounds each. I guess we had it coming. We knew the risks. And there's no point complaining about being eaten by a horse if you've agreed to play polo.

Many like myself have now fallen from a great financial height, and we received little sympathy as we crash-landed in a gorse bush in which a family of porcupines was nesting. It was a chastening experience. If the economy could be powered by gloating, the collapse of so many big financial institutions would have trigged an economic boom overnight.

As it is, however, the world economy is now officially, according to the International Monetary Fund, in a 'USC scenario' – in other words, Up Shit Creek. What is more, it has sold its paddle in return for the promise of two golden paddles in the future. So now it sits, lost in the uncharted slurry of that malodorous waterway, in an ostentatious, oversized speedboat, desperately gunning its broken engine and sending up distress flares to any watching government.

It remains to be seen whether or not the world will consolidate all of its various bank collapses, stock market pratfalls, unemployment capers and house price plummets into one gigantic international depression. Either way, the next few years are going to be a lot of fun for anyone who loves financial uncertainty.

At least, on a positive note, the crisis has introduced top-level economics to a new generation of fans. Leading figures from the financial world have been thrust to the forefront of public attention as never before, and a generation of impressionable young children will have been inspired by seeing their fiscal heroes on TV. They will now not want to be footballers, train drivers or televised karaoke stars when they grow up, but dream of becoming a Finance Minister, a member of the Bank of England Monetary Policy Committee, a Hedge Fund manager or a general economic guru.

Looking back now in the cold light of redundancy, I understand that the Credit Crunch had in fact been looming inescapably over the financial world like the bacon industry over a baby pig (albeit a pig that could have known it was coming if it had taken its snout out of its trough for a couple of minutes here and there).

The good times could not last for ever, because in essence the whole unappetising package of global economics has been an intermittently lucrative modern-day form of witchcraft, only with limousines instead of broomsticks, even more cackling, and the tacit approval of the Church – and

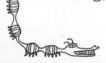

no chance of the perpetrators even coming close to being dunked in a pond. We allowed the entire financial stability of the world to depend upon a dangerously addictive cocktail of hypothetical bits of paper, made-up words, things that don't exist, guesswork and the mercurial confidence of stock market tricksters.

Many have suspected for some time that this would prove unsustainable in the long term. That suspicion is no longer a creeping one. It is prancing like a randy stallion on his first day at a stud farm. We took our eye off the ball, and now we've worn one on the nose.

I suppose, on reflection, we all knew deep down that the bubble of prosperity which so many of us have enjoyed in recent decades would eventually burst. We were merely hoping that it would not do so until after we were dead. But burst it has, as bubbles sometimes do. 2008 may have been the Chinese year of the rat; it has also been the economic year of the chickens coming home to shit their roosts.

So there can have been no better time in history to publish a book about the 2008 world financial crisis than now. A catastrophic global economic meltdown threatens the livelihoods of every single one of the 6.8 billion potential readers of this tome. This book is relevant to all of us. And its author can boast the same level of ignorance and confusion about these matters as I and my colleagues have displayed. He is an apposite guide through the swamp of confusion.

Finally, I would like to thank all the speculators, short-sellers, profiteers, gamblers, sharks, chancers, nincompoops, charlatans, fools, knights of the realm and millionaires such as myself who have made this book possible by generating The Crunch. We have introduced the subtle delicacies and thrilling plot twists of macroeconomics to a brand new audience, and we have brought a bit of front-page glamour to the grey world of finance. You are all very welcome.

Happy reading.

Sir Redvers Pook MBE.

"Is there anyone on board who knows how to fly a plane?"

**Elaine Dickinson (Julie Hagerty),
Airplane!, 1980**

"Uhh, uh-huh, yeah. It's all about the Benjamins, baby. Now what y'all wanna do? [sic]"

**Puff Daddy,
It's All About The Benjamins, 1998**

"It is well enough that people of the nation do not understand our banking and monetary system, for if they did, I believe there would be a revolution before tomorrow morning."

Henry Ford, car fan, 1863-1947

"Don't let your mouth write no check that your tail can't cash."

Bo Diddley, blues legend, 1928-2008

<u>IMPORTANT DISCLAIMER</u>

THE QUESTIONS IN THIS BOOK WERE
SUBMITTED BY COMPUTER-GENERATED
MEMBERS OF THE PUBLIC. THEIR
QUESTIONS HAVE BEEN ANSWERED TO
THE BEST OF THE AUTHOR'S ABILITY.
THE AUTHOR HAS NO BACKGROUND IN
ECONOMICS.

Does anything eat bankers?

Harrietta Stork, 6, child, Market Scarborough

FOR CENTURIES IT HAS been assumed that the banker had no natural predator. Traditionally bankers have been low-profile, tame beasts who shun human company out of fear and embarrassment, and whose natural life-caution makes them extremely careful in zoos and wildlife parks, thus minimising the risk of accidents.

However, recent events have shown previously unknown behavioural patterns amongst several species of banker. It transpires that many bankers, when left in unattended, unregulated markets, can turn feral and embark on ravenous sprees in which they risk their and others' livelihoods to gorge themselves on vulnerable financial institutions.

Furthermore, evidence has come to light that bankers do, when the mood takes them, resort to monetary cannibalism – there is independently verified footage of banks swallowing other banks whole, before spewing them out a short time later, lying on the ground, and whimpering to the government for help.

Following these revelations, bankers have also been fed to the tabloid press, which had previously shown little interest in them as a potential news source. The recent spectacular crises have shown that bankers can, in fact, provide valuable 'newstrients' to satisfy a tabloid's hunger.

The behaviour of bankers has always been baffling, and increasingly has become almost completely alien to us. However, whilst we can find it near impossible relate to them, the latest scientific research shows that ordinary human beings do in fact share 70 per cent of the same DNA as bankers. We are, it seems, much more closely related than anyone had previously thought.

What should I do if I find myself being chased by a banker?

Paul Small, 33, elbow surgeon,
Hackney Marshes

THERE IS SOME DISPUTE over the best course of action in this unfortunate but common circumstance. Some suggest you should stand still, others advise running in a zig-zag, others advocate climbing a tree.

The most important thing is not to show the banker any hint of financial vulnerability – they can sense it from several miles away, and once the scent is in their nostrils, they will hound and pester you mercilessly until you take a loan out with them, at which point they will slowly savage you

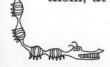

limb from financial limb. And never look bankers directly in the eye. They will gore your soul.

I always thought banking was boring. How wrong was I?

Colin Lunch, 44, freelance fire risk analyst,
Norwich-on-Sea

V<small>ERY.</small>

Er, yup. So how come banking has suddenly become so lethally risky that the government has now officially classified it as an extreme sport?

Colin Lunch, 44, freelance fire risk analyst,
Norwich-on-Sea

F<small>OR MILLENNIA, BANKING WAS</small> commonly thought of as the preserve of dull, safety-first, bean-counting squares who only did the job because of their inexplicable enjoyment of skull-crushing tedium.

However it now transpires that the banking community, far from being the buttoned-up epitome of conversational minimalism and the straight-laced safeguard of stability that we all assumed it to be, has in fact been playing financial Russian roulette with the entire world's economic wellbeing.

This revelation has shocked the planet to its molten core. It has been like finding out that your next-door neighbours Marjorie and Dennis, both aged 55 and active members of the local Crown Green Bowls club, are in fact the ex-Presidents of a bit of Yugoslavia and are about to take a very long unpaid sabbatical in The Hague; or that your local library, in addition to its core lending-and-fining business, has been running a satanic book-defacing cult, in which the staff gather in a woodland clearing, strip buck naked, date stamp each other's buttocks, and scrawl anti-monarchist graffiti all over the collected works of Anthony Trollope.

The culture shift began when banks realised they had achieved a level of trustworthiness that was so far beyond suspicion as to give them free license to have a bit of fun on the side with their customers' money. Thus began the dangerous addiction to safety-harness-free lending that has led to today's crisis. Chucking mortgages and loans around with the gayest of abandons was a huge adrenaline rush for ordinary bankers, who were more used to shunting grandma Doris's giro cheques around her current accounts like an unwanted pea around a fat child's plate.

High street banks began behaving increasingly tittishly towards their customers, offering their savers lower rates of interest than a 50-volume encyclopaedia of socks, and fining them for being financially unsuccessful – when Muddy Waters bluesily mused that "you can't lose what you never had", he had clearly never been £1 over his overdraft limit for twenty minutes.[1] Banks of course defend such charges by claiming that they are, in their own quirky way, simply encouraging people to be wealthier. Their critics respond that fining people for overdrawing themselves is akin to a sports teacher punishing a slow child for coming last in a running race by thwacking him repeatedly in the kneecaps with a monkey wrench whilst screaming at him to try harder. The banks win the argument by retorting that it's a free country, they can do what they like, and who are you to tell them how to live their lives?

In summary, the banking sector has cocked several king-sized luxury snooks at the world,

---

1 In a further blot on Waters's already minimal reputation as a financial adviser, the Credit Crunch has now proved conclusively that: (a) you quite clearly can lose what you never had; (b) you can also lose what no-one ever had; and (c) the time has come to try to stop losing stuff as a general rule. Waters may have been the 'Father of Chicago Blues', and to listen to a single wordless murmur of his voice may be to imbibe liquefied elemental truth, but the time has come to reassess the economic reliability of his lyrics.

safe in the knowledge that it is so important to the smooth running of modern society that governments will always be there to catch them when they fall, jump or are pushed off their financial Beachy Heads.

I know exactly what will happen to me on a month-to-month basis because I read my horoscope. So would it not have been possible for someone, somewhere, to have predicted this crisis?

Maradona Smith, 22, dog coiffeuse, Notting Hill

YES, BUT ONLY BY someone with one or more of the following rare qualities: foresight; hindsight (based on knowledge of the world's previous economic bungles); or a rudimentary grasp of basic arithmetic. No-one else, alive or dead, could possibly have predicted this economic house of cards would come crashing down like an elephant on a wedding cake, and unfortunately, no-one had either the foresight or hindsight to use any foresight or hindsight. Such is life.

Some of the greatest brains in the economics universe have claimed they had no way of knowing that the problems of 2008 would happen. Others

argue that they would have given themselves a better chance if they hadn't been locked in a special golden dungeon rolling around in 100-dollar bills and gurgling like well-fed babies.[2]

In some ways, the financial markets have displayed the same complacency and lack of prudence as the dinosaurs, who completely failed to prepare for an asteroid attack which they ought to have been able to predict from the existing geological evidence available to them and the balance of probability. Instead they thought to themselves: "Hey, we've had this planet stitched up for 150 million years now, and I've got big teeth. What could possibly go wrong?" So they smugly swanned around, roaring, eating cavemen and trying to get off with Raquel Welch, until, sure enough: Whack. Hello Dr Asteroid, goodbye Johnny Dinosaur.

---

2 See Appendix 1 for confirmation of whether or not they could have foreseen these problems.

A mate of mine in the pub told me the problem is that the whole financial world has suddenly got the jitters because of the sudden and belated realisation that, while there appears to be a lot of money in the world, almost none of that money actually exists. Is this true?

Derek Scrotch, 25, ATM analyst, Macclesfield

Yes. Most money is pretend. This has come about because banks realised that they could exploit their reputation as dullards to lend out around 30 times the amount of money they actually own without anyone raising an eyebrow, let alone an objection.

Furthermore, the bank you borrow your money from has itself probably borrowed that money from another bank, which in turn will have borrowed from another bank, and so on. This process is theoretically infinite, meaning that when you take a loan out, what you receive is, in essence, homeopathic money – it contains barely a trace of the original cash, but supposedly has the same function. Some experts claim that it works just as well as hard currency. Others are convinced that it is logically and practically such hogwash that you could clean a stadium full of pigs with it.

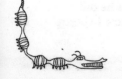

To my admittedly untrained head, that seems an odd way of doing things. How come this has come about?

Hadrian Stoop, 63, breakfast accessory inventor, Twickenham

THE ORIGINS OF THIS form of alternative finance can be traced back to Biblical times. The recently discovered and as yet unpublished 'Gospel According To Alvin' offers a radical new version of one of Jesus H. Christ's most famous miracles. The story goes that Jesus, then in his late 20s or early 30s, had just finished a particularly long and involved new parable in front of a sold-out 5,000-strong audience at an outdoor festival gig.[3] He noticed that his crowd was looking quite tired and hungry[4] and so, in lieu of his usual 'Dead

---

3 This was a three-and-a-half hour epic entitled 'The Parable Of The Tall But Unpopular Man', the fundamental message of which is that, just because you have long arms, you do not have to use them to smash people in the face. It is thought to have been a satire on the heavy-handed violence of Roman imperialism. Had this parable been published in one the four A-list gospels, it might have been able mollify modern-day American foreign policy.

4 "And the audience was bored. And Saleph who was from Jericho did heckle Jesus, and said unto him, 'Oi, Jesus, get off. That was self-indulgent rubbish, Jesus. You've lost your edge.' But Jesus refrained from telling Saleph that he did not come down to where he worked and tell him how to clean

Mouse Live Mouse' encore, he promised to give the crowd the five loaves of sliced white and two whole cod from his dressing room (his contractual rider at all of his major shows by this stage of his career).

He then buttered four of the loaves, filleted and mashed the fish, and shaped it into thin rectangles which he then covered with breadcrumbs from the fifth loaf. After a quick whizz in the frying pan, Jesus lent a fishfinger sandwich to each of his twelve disciples (even Thomas, who was vegan, and Andrew, who had hated the smell of fish ever since being shoved into an aquarium on a school trip). The self-proclaimed Son of God told the apostles to pay him back whenever they could, hopped on his magic donkey, winked at the crowd, and skedaddled.

The devout dozen, being good Christian men, felt guilty about being the only ones with food in an increasingly bemused, ravenous and restless congregation. Therefore, each disciple lent his fishfinger sandwich to a member of the audience. Inspired by this example, those spectators then passed their food on to the people sitting next to them, who in turn lent it to the people next to them, and so on, and so on. Eventually, twelve people

toilets. For he was merciful, and believed his new parable to be artistically valid." Alvin 14:12.

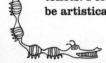

18

sat in the back row were left clutching somewhat soggy and misshapen fishfinger sandwiches, while each of the remaining 4,988 people in the capacity crowd was owed one fishfinger sandwich.

In this way, although technically Jesus did not actually feed the 5,000, he did enable them all to go home knowing that they were one fishfinger sandwich in credit, which they could call in whenever they felt like a snack. Though by no means his most impressive piece of magic, its value as a PR exercise was incalculable in terms of raising Jesus's profile.[5] Furthermore, and of greater long-term consequence, the Middle East's then number-1-ranked messiah had invented the principles of modern banking.

---

5 Experts consider this 'miracle' to have been second only to crucifixion in terms of increasing public awareness of what St Peter used to refer to as "Brand Jesus".

Well done him. But, with some of that hindsight you mentioned, was it really wise to base the entire financial stability of the world on pretend money?

Iche Onyebeli, 30, oil pipeline designer, Lagos

IT IS BEGINNING TO appear to have been at best a mistake, possibly even a blooper, and at worst full-blown gaffe – and one which could been avoided with the occasional application of what is known to the layman as "basic common sense".

However, for a long time the financial world successfully and lucratively relied on a common sense-averse approach. Clever financiers realised that traditional values of economy, such as balancing the books, long-term planning and mathematics, were not only "hideously outdated throwbacks to the pre-Christian era that can cut profits by up to 2000 per cent", but were also "really boring", and, more damagingly, "square".[6]

---

6 Mr J, an unnamed fund manager, reported to the House Of Commons Sub-Committee On Bullying In The Financial Services Sector: "I was mercilessly teased by my colleagues, friends and bosses when I raised concerns about the safety of an investment in ice cream futures. Mr X [a company executive, Mr J's immediate superior] humiliated me in front of the rest of my office – he put my jacket on, then mimicked me talking in a high-pitched whine about how I didn't want

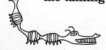

It was a classic Emperor's New Clothes scenario, only with money instead of clothes. In the famous fairy story, the emperor's plums-out attire sparked a craze for non-existent clothing, and people rushed out to buy the very latest in nudey fashions. However, come winter, when everyone became bored of the embarrassment at parties of wearing the same non-thing as someone else, a panic spread through the imaginary clothes market, and everyone tried to sell their non-existent garments at the same jumble sale. They all lost a lot of money, and realised that they had not been quite as smartly dressed as they had told each other. And the moral of the story is: always check the label.

Now the economic system has all but run out of imaginary money, and governments are reluctant to pretend to print any more of it, fearing they could risk further devaluing the original imaginary money that is still in circulation. Others claim that injecting a new tranche of money that is even

---

to take any risks in case my pencil broke, whilst mincing around and crying like a baby. He then made me eat a whole tub of ice cream as the rest of the staff encircled me, goading me to eat it faster and faster until I got a really bad headache. He then kicked me off my chair, put a wafer in my hair and licked my cheeks while everyone else chanted Buy, buy, buy, buy, buy.' What was I supposed to do? I gave in, and bought £15 million in ice cream futures based on the next day's weather forecast being quite good. It rained, and my client lost £14.8 million. But I had gained the respect of my colleagues, and that was all that mattered to me at the time."

more imaginary than the imaginary money that has been lost could make the latter seem more real again by comparison, and thus increase, or at least undecrease, in value.

As a general rule, dealing with things that exist is usually easier that dealing with things that do not. This is why snooker is played with physical balls rather than metaphorical ones.

SECRETS OF THE BANKING INDUSTRY FACT BOX

- As part of their initiation, new recruits at America's top investment banks have to kill a baby seal by slamming its head repeatedly in a photocopier.
- Three out of four workers in the banking sector psych themselves up for work on Monday mornings by watching the opening battle scene from Saving Private Ryan.
- 96% of retired professional footballers who have turned to a career in banking describe the feeling of selling a mortgage to a first-time buyer as being "better than scoring the winning goal in the cup final whilst making sweet love to that woman from The Manageress."
- During their lunch breaks, the staff in all major high street banks congregate in the secure

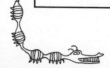

vaults, lock themselves in, open the safes, tip all the money into a giant paddling pool, strip to their regulation bank-issue underwear, and writhe around like snakes chanting, "Money, money, money, I've got cash on my tummy."

- The real reason why high street banks traditionally observe such insultingly unhelpful opening hours is because in the 1930s, the halcyon era of bank robberies, 68% of all stick-ups occurred before 9.30am and after 4.30pm. Most robbers were part-time in those days, and would perform their crimes on the way home to or from work.

- Schnauthauß-McGraw is the biggest Anglo-German banking conglomerate in the world, but in order to avoid having to pay tax in either country, its official headquarters are situated on a rubber dinghy bobbing around in the North Sea, staffed by a single receptionist in a wetsuit. Its chief executive Hermann Horstrubesch was born on a Tuesday, and makes every single one of his staff bake him a weekly cake on Monday evenings. The winner of the Tuesday morning cake-tasting is given the afternoon off from banking.

- Some bankers feel so guilty about their industry's role in the recent worldwide economic downturn that they need an extra coffee before they start work.

My pet Labrador Wendell, 8, has no concept of stopping eating when he has had enough. How come the financial markets have the same level of intellectual maturity and self-control as a fat, uncomfortable dog?

Crawl Sczepapankski, 40, house-husband, Ashwell

T HE PROBLEM IS THAT greed, like table tennis, is inherently competitive. Human beings, particularly those who work as bankers, generally want only two things: more, and more. This can be illustrated by the following statement by an anonymous high-level banking chief executive, given to a House Of Commons Sub-Committee in August 2008:

HOUSE OF COMMONS™ SUB-COMMITTEE ON CORPORATE GREED AND GENERAL FINANCIAL TWATTERY

Statement by Sir ████████████, MBE, OBE, DSO

20 August 2008

These things just get out of control before you know it. It's like when you're collecting solid gold statues of British weather forecasters: if you have just bought a giant golden statue of

the BBC's former badminton international Helen Willetts for £50 million, inevitably you will then want to buy a giant golden statue of ITV's surfing enthusiast Becky Mantin for £80 million, otherwise your friends and peers will think you have fallen on hard times.

They would come up to you in the sauna at Claridge's or somewhere and ask: 'How come you haven't bought a massive golden statue of a weather forecaster recently?'

You would reply: 'Oh, no reason. I'm perfectly happy with my Willetts. I think one giant golden meteorologist is enough.'

'Oh,' they would respond, sceptically. 'Oh. Really? Are you sure about that, Sir ████████? It's just that ████ has got an Isobel Lang and two Sarah Wilmshursts. So...'

'So what?'

'Look, mate, if you're having problems...'

'No, I'm fine.'

'Fine? You don't look fine. You've only got one giant golden weather forecaster. That's not 'fine' in my book.'

'OK, I'll get the Mantin. And a Philip Avery. For the wife.'

You see? That's how it all spirals out of control. But that's capitalism – these kinds of thing have trickledown benefits for ordinary people. Give it 20 years, there will be stalls on every street corner selling affordable, low-quality porcelain Carol Kirkwoods that everyone can own. So, indirectly, we are helping small business. We are. We <u>are</u>. Can I go now?

A swift examination of the world's most successful sports stars reveals that there is a fine line between confidence and arrogance, with heroes on one side and dicks on the other. On which side of that line has the financial world been standing?

Mike Twelve, 28, hypnosalesman, Sunderland

BOTH SIDES. IT IS indeed a fine line. Fine, and easily straddleable. The financial world tiptoed along it for some time; now it has slipped and fallen, and the line is giving it the painful wedgie it deserves. It has behaved like an economic version of the young mythological Greek lad, Icarus. With his father Daedalus, the celebrity labyrinth designer, Icarus used special wax wings to effect an ambitious aerial jailbreak from HMP Knossos in Ancient Crete.

Tragically the boy, with an over-confidence stemming from a mixture of youth and a lack of knowledge of physics, ignored his old man's warnings not to fly too close to the sun. Sure enough, his wings melted and, flap as he might, the youngster smash-landed in the sea, copping some fatal injuries.

His death was not pointless, however – he became immortalised as a symbol of the dangers of overreaching ambition, he still retains the world record for highest altitude attained on wax wings, and, perhaps most importantly, he also helped improve aircraft safety. Thanks to him, most of the world's leading airlines now use metal, rather than wax, wings. Without Icarus, it is doubtful that air travel would be popular, or indeed legal.

The financial markets (having clearly only read the first half of the story) have acted in a similar way to Icarus, but taken his efforts a couple of steps further. Their modern-day Icarus didn't approach the sun because he just wanted to fly as high as possible. He wanted to stick a flag in the sun, claim ownership of it, then sell it, and buy it back again at a knockdown rate after forcing its price down by leaking a rumour that it was about to run out of fire. And then, after safeguarding his own pension and pay-off, cause the sun to go bankrupt, and make the rest of us live in the dark.

I would feel better about the world's current economic mess if I could blame someone or something for it. Someone should take the rap – and I want to give them that rap. I've got the severed finger of blame in a blood-splattered envelope postmarked 'Credit Crunch'. Into whose letterbox should I post it?

'Boston' Fred Socks, 50, salami developer, Boston

SCIENCE AND HISTORY HAVE both proved that the human soul is genetically programmed to blame someone else in times of crisis. It is a basic psychological defence mechanism that is the human evolutionary equivalent of a porcupine sticking its quills out. And the blame for the failure of the banks has been thrown around like a 92-year-old woman who inadvertently entered a professional wrestling tournament.

Amongst the potential candidates to be blamed for their roles in one of the biggest, silliest and most irresponsible games of all time are:

- **The Capitalists** – for failing to look at the economic cheese trolley and say to the waiter, "Well it looks delicious, but I think I've had enough. That pudding finished me off."
- **The Communists** – if they hadn't kicked off

the whole left-wing/right-wing dick-swinging contest, then capitalism wouldn't have felt the need to prove how tough it is by swinging a dick that wasn't its to swing through a plate glass window it could not afford to fix.

- **The Ancient Greeks** – things were going fine until they distracted themselves from the serious business of establishing western civilisation by getting naked, oiling up, and wrestling boys.

- **Disgraced sprinter Ben Johnson** – the Canadian sullied the purity of the Olympic ideal, and thus set a precedent of moral naughtiness that many in the financial sector followed. If our athletic heroes could not maintain basic moral standards, why should our banks and traders?

- **Satan** – America, playing the lead role in this unfunny comedy of errors, is a good Christian country, and as such could never have sunk so low had the devil himself not been interfering.

- **Women who have abortions, and the doctors who carry them out** – the pro-life movement could have saved the world from economic meltdown, if only people had been prepared to listen to them. Because if more people had had more children, they would have had less money, and therefore would have been even less able to afford to buy houses they already could not afford. At some point the sub-prime mortgage sellers would have had to say 'no' to someone, and as a result the crisis would have been marginally less bad.

- **Al Qaeda** – their dastardly deeds left the western world with no choice but to launch a series of financially ruinous wars that destabilised the global economy. A real bunch of rotters.

- **Actor Dan Ackroyd** – only too happy to profit from the markets in fictional 1983 film Trading Places, but eerily quiet on the subject of impending stock market slumps in the more important real world.

- **The British government** – happy to be taken for nice tasty picnics by big business, until the bill from the delicatessen landed on Downing Street's doormat.

- **Fat Cat bonuses** – widely castigated for being too big, too offensive and still too big, whereas in reality, the problem was that the bonuses were not big or offensive enough. If the bonuses had been in the billions instead of the millions, the world might have woken up and smelt that the coffee machine was on fire a little bit sooner.

- **You** – when times were good, were you

writing daily letters to your MP warning about the dangers of economic short-termism and unregulated profiteering? If not, it is, at least partially, your fault.

* **The advertising industry** – its decades-long campaign to render people unable to distinguish a good offer from an obvious trap has proven to be devastating by the sub-prime crisis.

I hate having to make a choice. Can you not just tell me who is <u>actually</u> to blame?

Aluf Masnuka, 60,
fire alarm test scheduler, Bristol

[Answer removed pending legal proceedings. A case is being brought by Our Children's Children And Our Children's Children's Children Ltd, a charitable trust set up to represent the interests of our children's children and any subsequent generations of children that may follow. OCCOCCC is seeking financial compensation payable to the people of the future, claiming that the actions and inactions of the late 20th- and early 21st-century world will have left the planet virtually uninhabitable, almost bankrupt, and essentially pointless within 100 years.

Almost every major political and commercial institution in the world is mentioned in the indictment, along with several billion individual citizens, with accusations ranging from irresponsible financial short-termism, via environmental ostrichism, rubbish architecture and needless eating, all the way to outright government theft from the coffers of the future. The case, which is being heard at Huntingdon Magistrates' Court, is expected to run for at least 40 years. The likely appeal which will follow the verdict means that the answer to this question will remain classified until 2108 at the earliest.]

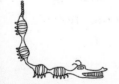

The current financial hullabaloo has set the world's markets frantically pressing the panic button like a physics student on a University Challenge team losing by 50 points with two minutes left, trying to pre-emptively answer a question about the molecular structure of magnesium tetrachloride. But what exactly has prompted governments the world over to whip their biggest available novelty chequebooks out of their special emergency drawers?

Thompson McNulty, 30, professional scuffle re-enactor, Liverpool-on-Thames

THE WORLD'S POLITICAL AND economic leaders worked around several clocks in their efforts to deliver a bail-out – any bail-out – to the spluttering banks. They have left no brow unfurrowed in their determination to show the millions of potential voters and customers afflicted by the crisis that they really do care.

To the uninitiated brain, using public money for multi-billion-pound bail-outs may seem to be the political equivalent of slaughtering a bull on a hastily constructed polystyrene altar, looking skywards, and saying, "Well then, Zeus, how about it? Eh? Zeus? Zeus? Are you there, Zeus? Zeus. Could you get back to us on that one? ASAP please. Amen."

However, Sir Isaac Newton's First Law Of Economics states that if you throw enough money at a problem, some of it will stick.[7]

Nevertheless, the term 'bail-out' is of considerable concern. Its two principal meanings offer little comfort to the natural sceptic. A 'bail-out' seems destined to leave either:

---

7 Newton's early work shows his first strides towards this theory. In 1661, aged 18, the physics hall-of-famer wrote in his self-published Scientifical, Philosophicant and Economicalist Musings Of A Teenage Genius: "My humble experience on the semi-professional food-fighting circuit informs me that, when throwing a substance with the intention of it sticking to an object, what precise object the substance sticks to is a matter of little or no import – it is better for something to stick to something, than for nothing to stick to anything. As it is with food, so it is with money, and with paint, and with the mud of rumour. This was a lesson well learnt in my losing quarter-final at the Bubonix Plague Remedies East Anglian Masters last Whitsuntide, when my careful, strategic accuracy with profiteroles was of scant utility against the splattering, splurging, blancmange bombardment which disgorged itself all around me like the warm, engulfing vomit of a chundering dragon, from the hands of my rightful vanquisher, Sir Tredwell 'Helicopter Arms' Ploughwick. He completed his dominion of me by leaping off a pommel horse, ululating in his well-beknownst Viking style, and hurling an apple from on high onto the crown of my quivering, pudding-smirched bonce. 'Why,' I wondered in my moment of ultimate drubbing, 'did that fruit hurt quite so much? Seemingly slightly more than the projectile power of Ploughwick's arm alone would merit. Why, I wonder, why?'"

34

1. an aeroplane-load of passengers peering with increasing anxiety out of their windows at their rapidly descending ex-pilot, contemplating how difficult it must be to land a large commercial aircraft without prior training, and, more pressingly, to do so safely; or

2. a boat-load of wet-socked passengers admiring the frantic intensity of the crew's bucketwork, whilst wondering how wide an ocean is, and what is actually being done to plug the big hole in the hull.

Both possibilities portend an at-best uncomfortable economic journey ahead, and at worst a rapid crash or slow sinking, ending in disaster and recrimination.

As bail-out after bail-out was approved by twitching, fidgety governments, ordinary bankrupt gamblers the world over must have smiled ruefully at the quirky inconsistencies of life and thought to themselves: "It could have been me. If only I had been a bank instead of a drunken punter, I could have been saved from the consequences of my own reckless flutters." Because the current crisis appears to be the result of the World Economy essentially walking into a casino and placing the entire monetary wellbeing of the planet on red, all the while muttering to itself: "I've got a system, I've got a system."

When you see a depressed and lonely old man staggering away from his local turf accountant, re-lighting half a rolled-up cigarette and wondering what his ex-wife is up to these days, you can comfort yourself with the knowledge that (a) at least it is his own money he has wasted, and (b) at least the horse he blew it on actually existed. Neither of these consolations applies to failed banks.

Indeed, the starkly divergent government attitudes and reactions to these different forms of failed gambling proves, once again, Newton's Second Law Of Economics: that it is genuinely amazing what you can get away with if you are wearing a good-quality suit.

I'm having a few cash flow problems too, just like a bank. I'd quite like the Government to bail me out. How do I qualify?

Kit Carr, 52, road junction designer, Erdinton

IF YOU CAN CONVINCE the government that your economic survival is essential to the wellbeing of the nation, they will do everything within their power to prevent your demise. Hence the Queen Mother was kept alive through weekly infusions of virgin's blood until 1999 when, at the supernatural

age of 98, she died not especially peacefully in a wheelchair race against her arch nemesis Thora Hird, on the A303 near Andover.

However, fearing that her death would have a catastrophic impact on national morale, the government covered up this conclusive proof of her royal mortality, projecting a hologram of Her Royal Agedness at occasional public appearances and frequent race meetings until 2002, by which time her presence had come to be thought of as an historical anomaly in a thrusting new millennium. She was then gradually phased out over several months.

Essentially, the failing banks issued coded threats that, if they were allowed to fail, they would take the livelihoods of thousands of innocent bystanders with them. This left the government in a classic Catch £222 Billion situation.

You must also be considered too big to fail (see Appendix 3). When HBOS knocked on the Chancellor's window at 3 o'clock in the morning saying it had got itself into a bit of trouble, the government was only too keen to help. If Dave from Dave's Chimney Repair And Repointing Services were to do the same in his time of hardship, he would be arrested under the Prevention Of Terrorism Act (subsection 13.8, Interference Of VIP Sleep).

If you **do** succeed in being bailed out, and are partly or wholly nationalised, you must be prepared to accept that there are downsides to being owned by the State. The government can ask you to do menial tasks which you may consider beneath you, such as putting cones on motorways, fighting some Taleban, installing bugging devices in the hotel rooms of visiting diplomats, or putting a new roof on a school chemistry lab after the last one blew off in a botched experiment with copper sulphate.

In addition, you are vulnerable to a future change of government after an election or coup. The new administration may wish to stamp its own identity on national proceedings by randomly reversing the actions of its predecessors. Thus you could easily be privatised, and bought out by a company which sees you purely as a commodity from which to profit. You may end up feeling cheap, used and dirty – the privatised rail network, for example, has experienced the latter two of these three emotions.

Critics of the bail-outs have claimed that the government has essentially justified, or at least excused, corporate malpractice by providing a fallback for badly run businesses, thus setting a dangerous precedent. As famous circus owner Scranton Huke said at his trial for transgressions of workplace safety regulations: "If you take away the safety net, you will find that your tightrope walkers and trapeze artists concentrate considerably harder."

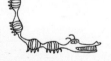

When talking about their bailout packages, politicians have been bandying around numbers of which neither I nor anyone in my extended family has ever heard. How much is this all going to cost in the end?

Julius Grudge, 46,
professional paintballer, Swansea

SOME ESTIMATE THE OVERALL cost of all the world's banking bailouts will top the $3 trillion mark on the Credit Crunch totaliser.

The sums of money involved must boggle even the tiny minds of top-level footballers. In fact, with its $700 billion bail-out bonanza (part of the Bush administration's 'Fingers Crossed '08' campaign), the US Treasury could have afforded to buy footballer Christiano Ronaldo off Manchester United for £250 million and treble his current weekly wage, just to keep him chained to a radiator in a Washington dungeon for the next 20,000 years. That is real money.

It is also a viable transfer – the fee is three or four times what Real Madrid were offering in the summer of 2008, and, given that the US Treasury are not a rival club liable to knock the Red Devils out of the Champions League, United would almost certainly accept the offer. Ronaldo, for his part, would find the financial package extremely hard to turn down, since even a certified buffoon such as he would find this mega-wage sufficient. Plus it is a fact that everyone likes career stability, and 20,000-year contracts are increasingly rare in modern professional sport.

So the Portuguese starlet would almost certainly sign up, giving a press conference saying that he felt he had enjoyed his time at Old Trafford but had come to a point in his career at which he needed a new challenge, that being chained to a radiator in a US government dungeon offered him just that opportunity, and that he did not want to end his career thinking "What if?"; so he was delighted to sign, and that he looked forward to forming a productive partnership with both the chains and the radiator, both of which he has always rated very highly.

I can think of a lot of things I'd like to have spent two or three trillion bucks on that aren't speculatively trying to rescue the world's naughty banking sector. But I know this isn't all about me. If the world's governments had wanted a guaranteed return on their investment, what else could they have flung this money at?

Lox Bagel, 58, personal insult attorney,
New York City

- The development of a personal satellite missile defence system to protect individual citizens from rogue states. This should form part of a broader programme of decentralising national security and defence – giving choice to the taxpayer, enabling people to decide for themselves how much of a threat they face, and whether to allocate their own personal security budget to missile defence, covert intelligence, or preemptive military action. The device could easily be adapted by DIY enthusiasts to provide protection against wasps, heralding a bold new era of carefree picnicking.
- The environment. Love it or hate it, it's here to stay, and it's becoming stroppier by the year. Being given a couple of trillion dollars is a

life-changing experience for most people and institutions, apart from the banking sector, for whom it is a life-preserving one. For the environment, it would be a mind-blower – the spectacle of environmental research scientists cartwheeling around their laboratories in celebration at being able to afford more than one new test tube a year would be worth the ticket price on its own.

A multi-trillion bailout package for the ecosystem would enable all of the following projects:

- The development and design of an electric car that (a) works, (b) looks cool, and (c) makes enough noise. One of the principal objections to the electric car, other than its potentially catastrophic effect on the oil industry,[8] has been how much worse it is for impressing girls than a conventional carbon-fuelled vehicle. Once an electric car can be aggressively revved to the requisite decibel level, this significant caveat will be largely overcome.

---

8 For those who view the oil industry as a giant profiteering behemoth, it should be noted that many others would suffer in the event of the electric car becoming popular. It would lead, for example, to a significant downturn in the sales of sweets in motorway service stations, resulting in the loss of jobs in both the manufacturing and retail sectors of the confectionery industry.

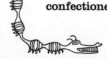

An alternative would be to devote this tranche of research funding to genetically modifying horses to make them faster, more reliable in cold weather, with greater stamina and GPS compatibility, with a view to them resuming their rightful place as mankind's premier form of transport.[9]

- A multi-billion-pound advertising campaign to convince people that wind farms actually look OK. In fact, they are quite majestic in their own way.

- Development of new alternative energy sources. Attempts should be made to harness the power of sexual tension, renowned as one of the most potent untapped forms of energy in the world, particularly in Britain where traditionally it is pent up. There are hundreds of thousands of teenage boys in this country, and several thousand female French teachers. If those two marginalised social groups are ever hooked up to the same generator, the sparks will fly (albeit only in one direction[10]).

---

9 However, scientifically, the horse is a more carbon-naughty form of transport than the car. It produces significant amounts of carbon dioxide and methane from the various ends of its body, and its diet of hay and sugarlumps requires agriculture, which is one of the most ecodamaging activities of all and should therefore, objectively, be outlawed.

10 Therefore requiring the DC current generated to be converted into an AC current for household use.

- An extensive search of the world's ocean beds to find if there is a plughole somewhere that could counteract rising sea levels. This would save many lives. More importantly, it would also save many carpets. You can make new people. But carpets, you have to buy.

- A giant golden statue of Princess Diana. The bailout money could buy around 125,000 tonnes of gold. The Statue of Liberty weighs around 200 tonnes, and is 46 metres tall. If the Diana were made of nothing but gold, it could be 3,600 metres tall. If it were covered in a superficial gold cladding, just as the Statue of Liberty is clad in skimpy copper, it could be more than 26 kilometres tall – three times the height of Mount Everest, and visible from every single inhabited place on earth.

- A war with Iran. The Iraq war has cost around $750 billion. Iran is four times bigger than Iraq.

- Saving the world's children. According to UNICEF, £500 million could save the lives of a million children. This equates to £500 per kid, which may seem quite expensive – around the cost of a reasonable-quality plasma-screen television, which offers the consumer so much more entertainment and so many more functions than a sickly African infant. But at

this price, the bailout money could save 3.6 billion children's lives. This, however, presents logistical difficulties: UNICEF figures suggest that annual child mortality in sub-Saharan African and South Asia has fallen to around 8 million, so the bail-out money would have to be staggered to save all children over the next 450 years to ensure that none of it is wasted.

- 42 million motorboats. Reasonable quality ones, too. Everyone loves motorboats. The governments of the world could have clubbed their bail-out money together to make sure there was 1 motorboat per 168 people in the world, which would have entitled everyone on the planet to one hour's motorboating a week. Aside from the obvious boost this would give to the beleaguered motorboat manufacturing sector, it is impossible to claim that the world would not be a happier place under this scheme.

I'm not a government, but just in case I ever become one – or, heaven forfend, a member of one – how do I calculate exactly how big a bail-out should be?

Voracine Boss, 34, gastronomic physics expert, Lincoln

THIS IS A COMPLEX balancing act, which requires the perpetrating government to achieve at once the maximum appearance of action and the minimum loss of face. The overall package must also offer both a reasonable possibility of success and a guarantee that failure will not be immediate – a six-month delay is the minimum required to be able to foist any blame convincingly onto someone or something else.

It is important that a government aims for MCE (Maximum Conceivable Expenditure) in order to accentuate the apparent seriousness of the situation, and to avoid future accusations of not throwing enough money at the problem. This sum must be considerably higher than the current TOU (Threshold Of Unfathomability, the sum beyond which the human brain ceases to be able to comprehend quantities of money[11]).

---

11 The Threshold Of Unfathomability is a critical number in most economic calculations. It may vary according to its

If you do find yourself in a situation where you have to bail out a financial institution, whether that be a bank, a small business, or a daughter, the basic calculation should be: a sum that seems reasonable for the purpose, multiplied by a contingency factor of 10,000 per cent.

The British and American governments have spent roughly the same amount of money on bailing out their silly banks as they have on the Iraq War. Which is likely to prove the greater waste of money in the long term?

Patella Hink, 50, egg scrambling coach, Stoke

IT'S TOO EARLY TO say, but it looks all set to be a titanic battle, the Nadal-Federer of government spending. Only time will reveal whether they are

---

point in history and specific context – for example, paying £9.6 million for a shark in a formaldehyde tank may have been considered the height of folly and way beyond the TOU in the 19th century, whereas in the early 21st it is merely the going market rate, and only slightly beyond the TOU. Similarly, earning $1 million for winning a two-hour cricket match is beyond the TOU of right-thinking people, but comfortably within it for tycoons. As a general rule, if an amount of money contains more digits than two human hands, it is beyond the TOU. The official TOU is viewed by historians as a reliable gauge of a society's obsession with wealth.

hitting the nail on the head with the bailouts, or hitting the nail with their heads, before clutching their faces and complaining that the nail was pointier than the expert advice had warned. Similarly, only time will reveal whether the weapons of mass destruction in Iraq really existed.[12]

On the positive side, should Iraq eventually settle into peaceful, stable democracy, the whole expensive expedition will have established to the world the exact number of wrongs that do actually make a

---

12 At time of going to print, in November 2008, this matter had still to be definitively resolved. It is possible that America's campaign was based on a faulty interpretation of an oracle – not the first such clanger to be dropped in military history. In the 6th century BC, Lydian king Croesus consulted the Delphic oracle about his forthcoming proposed invasion of Persia. The oracle told him that if he invaded, a great empire would fall. Croesus cockily forged ahead with his crack at the Persians, went down to a heavy away defeat, and died in the realisation that the great empire which had fallen was his own. So it was with the WMDs. When Delphi oracularised to the Pentagon (one of the ancient Greek site's few remaining subscribers) that Iraq possessed the potential to bring destruction to America, Rumsfeld and his chums wrongly assumed that this meant Saddam Hussein had, despite years of inspections, sanctions, bombing raids and covert surveillance, squirreled away some big old fireworks. It has since turned out that the oracle was in fact inferring that a war in Iraq could prove financially ruinous for the US economy, and create damaging resentment towards America that could take generations to heal. The full details will emerge when the official documents from Delphi and Washington are released in 2102. It is rumoured that when Rumsfeld later consulted the oracle over his proposed invasion of modern-day Persia (Iran), the oracle merely snorted and said, "Get real, big horse. Have you looked at it on a map?"

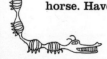

right. It is not yet known what this number will be, other than that it must be considerably more two.

It should also be remembered, with regard to the bailouts, that governments have asked for the money back eventually, and the banking sector replied, "Yeah, yeah, sure, whatever you want, mate," before scuttling off down an alley looking shifty. So in the long term, it will probably prove to have been an absolute bargain.

It seems to me that governments intervened a little too late. Shouldn't they have stuck their oar into this quagmire somewhat sooner?

Frank Limadia, 59, in-house instrument polisher,
Barnstaple Institute Of Trumpets

TIMING SUCH INTERVENTIONS IS difficult, but it now appears that the world's politicians did not so much grasp the economic bull by the horns as hide behind a phone box until the bull had charged into a crowded lingerie store, then emerge into the ensuing underwear-strewn mayhem brandishing a fake plastic Viking helmet and shouting: "Trust me, it's all under control."

If they had acted more swiftly, they would have been accused of interfering in the holy workings of the free market, of 'playing God' with the economy, as they were alleged to be doing when they voted on human-animal hybrid embryo research.

But the fact of the matter is that politicians do often play God – in that they are not believed in any more by the majority of the population, they have not done anything demonstrably useful for a very long time, and they keep employing members of their own family in important positions.[13] The resemblance is uncanny. They are playing God, and they're method acting to Brando standards.

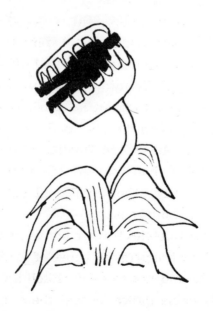

13 This is not to say that Jesus was not best man for the job, merely that it would have been reassuring if there had been a little more transparency in the recruitment process.

When it comes to panicking, the general rule of thumb in most walks of life seems to be: Don't – it won't help, and it will make you look like an idiot. So why is that the financial markets seem to aggressively soil themselves at the merest hint of a downward graph?

Graham Herdandez a.k.a. The Human Thermostat, 41, millionaire temperature-based entertainer, Monaco

P ANIC IS A CONTRARY little shit. It is an evolutionary reflex, a survival instinct which, more often than not, leads to disaster. From buffalos chasing each other off cliffs into the willing saucepans of prehistoric chefs, to financial markets stampeding towards oblivion on the basis of disappointing sales of toasters in Mike's Top Quality Kitchen Store in Ilkeston, panic has scarred the planet's history as much as any other irrational emotion, apart perhaps from smugness.

The recent wobblies thrown by the financial world illustrate how the primary cause of panic in human life is being told not to panic. Such an instruction is a 99%-reliable indicator that there is something afoot worth panicking about. No captain of a ship has ever, in the middle of an on-time, untroubled, iceberg-free Atlantic crossing, switched on the boat's public address system and barked, "Nobody panic. For god's sake, nobody panic. It's not going to help." If a zoo attendant were to grab you by the collar, shake you vigorously, and tell you at close facial quarters to "calm down", and that "everything's probably going to be OK as long as everyone keeps their cool", you would instantly assume that there was an escaped tiger on the loose, and not merely that penguin feeding time had been delayed by five minutes due to insufficient herring.

Therefore, the constant panic-fuelled and panic-fuelling speculation about the extent of the financial collapse has become a self-fulfilling prophecy.

Rumours have been a significant contributor to this. Stock markets have highly developed rumour-sensing organs, which can detect a five-second trace of a rumour in 10,000,000 square minutes of chat. A rumour, once detected and spread, soon has far more influence than a humble fact, because a fact remains the same-sized piece of truth no matter how often it is repeated, whereas a rumour can grow exponentially into a presumption, until it overwhelms all other relevant information and mutates into a panic.[14]

---

14 This further supports Einstein's First Law Of Tabloid Journalism, which states that if you print a lie in big enough letters, it becomes a fact.

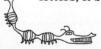

In these difficult times, it is incumbent upon all people in society to try to spread the kind of rumours which might have a positive impact on the confidence of the economy. In Britain, such whisperings might include:

- The Queen being pregnant again. Nothing boosts national morale like a good news story from Buckingham Palace.
- The Commonwealth letting Britain have a second crack at The Empire. They understand that Britain meant well last time, and that we would probably avoid some of the goofs and pratfalls that wound people up so much first time round.
- British scientists finding a way of converting sarcasm into electricity. This could make Britain the richest country in the world.

Unregulated rumours, no matter how well-meaning, have a tendency to spiral out of control (as proven by, for example, the history of organised religion). It would therefore be expedient for the government to create a new post in Cabinet for a Minister for Rumour-Mongering. The Minister would be responsible both for spreading positive innuendo about British social and economic matters, and for the international dissemination of idle tittle-tattle harmful to our rivals and enemies. This would officially formalise a system that is in effect already operational.

What is the optimum face for a politician to pull while talking about the credit crisis?

David Swimmer, 22, actress, Aberystwyth
National Theatre

THIS IS A DIFFICULT skill, but one which now forms a crucial part of the training at Politician School. The default facial posture of smug self-assurance, ready at any moment to break into braying cockishness, is suitable for most front-bench House of Commons badinage and Conference tub-thumping. But serious times call for serious faces.

In a wide-ranging crisis that affects large swathes of potential voters, the politician must display a delicate mixture of concern, authority and blamelessness.

The ideal face for this purpose requires:

- The chin to be tucked firmly into the neck to emphasise quite how especially seriously the matter is being taken, and that no partisan point-scoring frivolity will be indulged in;

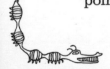

- The head to be cocked at a slight angle, but no more than 12 degrees from the perpendicular, to express sympathy and empathy without slipping into condescension;
- The brow to be at least 50 per cent furrowed, in order to convey that serious thought is being given to the matter, but that you are not cluelessly panicking with no idea how to react;
- The eyes to be open to a standard width – they should be neither too narrow (scornful) nor too wide (terrified); and
- The cheeks not to be puffed out – jowl inflation signifies that you are suffering wither from 'issue fatigue'[15] or a desire to mate, neither of which is what the public wishes to infer at such a time.

Also, resist the temptation to twist your ears and stick your tongue out to lighten the mood. Do not wink. Do not twitch your nose like a rabbit.

Overall, this almost identical to the face that should be pulled when listening to parents

---

15 Issue Fatigue is a condition that affects almost all politicians when a story has been in the news at least once every two days for more than a month. Symptoms include responding to a question about the issue by citing random statistics to prove how well (or badly) the government is performing in a completely unrelated area.

describing their child's failure to land one of the marquee roles in the school nativity play.

Whenever a politician issues a statement telling the nation or world exactly how badly mangled the economy is, the markets plunge like a fading film actress's neckline. We all know that honesty is not the best policy – if it were, politicians would surely be inclined to use it a bit more often – but is there an argument that, in times of economic crisis, it is in fact the worst?

Dinky Drinklestein, 65, anti-tennis protestor, Wimbledon

Yes. The escalating crisis was driven principally by politicians saying how bad things were, and the media reporting (a) how bad things were and (b) politicians saying how bad things were. If our leaders had had the political courage to lie when it was most needed, and our media had had the sense of public responsibility to run a full blackout on the economic problems, the situation would be far better today.

There is a time and place for truth, and neither

of them is on the cusp of a recession. Truth is a dangerous, potentially explosive substance, which must be applied with extreme care and precision. In a cost-cutting scheme, the government recently launched an NHS truth initiative, under which surgeons told hospital patients exactly how painful their surgery was going to be, in an effort to dissuade them from undergoing costly operations. This not only saved money, but also released valuable bed space and at the same time boosted the beleaguered funeral industry, which has been so adversely affected by advances in the fields of medical science, road safety and international diplomacy.

The workings of international finance seem awfully complicated and grown-up. Are they any of my business?

Deliverance Ponsford, 81, metal detective,
Melbourne, Australia

No. ADMITTEDLY, THEY DO affect you both directly and indirectly, but then so does the weather and you're not allowed to interfere with that, are you? Such matters are way beyond our control and comprehension. They are also, it transpires, way beyond the control and comprehension of the people whose specific job it is to control and comprehend them.

Therefore it is advisable, and perhaps essential, to pretend that these issues are someone else's problem. Leave them to the mysterious self-decapitating hydra that is world economics.

Additionally, whilst ignorance may be slightly overrated by those who consider it to be 'bliss', it does have its uses as a means of anger control when examining the world. A total lack of knowledge about global finance is the quickest and easiest way to overcome any doubts about its long-term dangers and ethical quirks. If you examine the financial system too closely, you will feel yourself being slowly overwhelmed by the same feelings of disgust, resentment and confusion you would experience when watching an electricity salesman saw off his own testicles all over your living-room carpet.

Ignorance has also made the build-up to the Credit Crunch more enjoyable. For years, some experts tried to alert us to the impending crisis. But we chose to ignore the warning signs, and thus managed to wangle ourselves a few bonus years of fun, stress-free spending before having to turn our attention to analysing exactly what had just hit the fan.

So, in summary: Yes, it is your problem, and therefore, no, it's none of your business. Butt out of it, big horse. Watch the golf. It's for your own

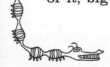

good. Ignore it, or you may soon find yourself wanting to swap places with Christopher Walken in the second half of The Deer Hunter.

Right. But is there anyone anywhere in the world who really knows exactly how the system works?

Enid Brighton, 68, author impersonator, Hull

Yes, of course, there are loads. It is a complex system but one well understood by those who—

Ah, ah, ah. Be honest. Is there anyone who knows what's going on?

Enid Brighton, 68, author impersonator, Hull

No. No one at all. This much has become excruciatingly obvious during the bail-out phase of the crisis. The world's biggest economic powers have been speculatively launching massive clods of money at the problem, and the world's leading economic experts, when asked whether this tactic will work, have replied: "Dunno mate. We'll just have to wait and see."

When pressed further, they have responded with

answers such as "Can't help right now, mate, I'm eating my ice cream", "Oh look, a puffin, don't see many of them at this time of year", and "What part of 'dunno' are you struggling to understand? Now get out of my face, or I will get you out of my face."

Perhaps the workings of the markets, like the laws of rugby union, are so mystical as to be truly unknowable even by those closest to them. It certainly seems increasingly likely that future generations will look upon modern economics with the same scorn and amusement as we now view medieval alchemy, and ask how could people believe in something so patently preposterous. Just as alchemists desperately searched for the philosopher's stone, a substance which could turn ordinary bits of metal into pure gold, so speculators developed the derivatives market for what amounted to the same purpose.[16]

---

16 It should be noticed that not all alchemists were lunatics in flamboyant hats. Isaac Newton was known enjoy a quick spot of alchemy in his spare time, and Carol Vorderman, his 21st-century equivalent, spends alternate weekends trying to create the elixir of life out of ordinary supermarket cordials. Although the philosopher's stone itself has never been found (correct at time of publication), there are rumours that football agents have found a substance which turns journeymen into cash cows; and Harry Potter inventor J.K. Rowling proved that a book with 'the philosopher's stone' in the title can turn words into millions and millions of pounds. So maybe the alchemists were barking up the right tree after all, but at the wrong cat.

Further testament to the enigmatic nature of finance comes from little Adam Smith who, in his 1776 economics blockbuster <u>The Wealth Of Nations</u>, wrote about "the invisible hand" guiding the market. In recent years, that invisible hand has been treating itself to more than the occasional unsolicited grope, as invisible hands inevitably will. It has also been flicking invisible v-signs at the general public. Many now argue that governments must step in and regulate the invisible hand – at least make it wear a glove so its unwanted fondlings can be seen, or even anticipated if it is obviously rubbing its fingers and thumb together with excessive excitement; or retrospectively punish it with a slap.

As far as I was concerned, 'short-selling' was an illegal transaction in the underground dwarf trade. It turns out to have brought the world economy to its knees, begging either for forgiveness or to be put out of its misery. So what is it really?

Mookie Chavez, 45, pinch violinist,
Baseball Orchestra Of Minnesota

SHORT-SELLING INVOLVES TRADING STOCK which isn't yours. You borrow some shares or derivatives, whatever they really are, from a broker, friend or uncle; you then flog them, anticipating that the price will fall, before buying them back on the cheap at a later juncture and handing them back to the owner saying, "There you are, good as new," as you pocket the difference between the two sales prices.

This practice is not restricted to stock market trading. For example, on arriving at the office in the morning, you may offer to look after your colleague's teatime egg sandwich. Whilst he or she isn't looking, you nip out of the office and sell the sandwich as a breakfast snack to a hungry commuter for the standard egg sandwich morning price of £2.50. You return to the office, whistling as if nothing has happened; then at

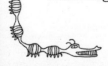

4pm, when your colleague is starting to look a bit peckish, you make an excuse for leaving the office, claiming that you have to buy a new dog for your next-door neighbour, or do a minute's exercise at the local gym, or that you are taking up smoking. You scurry to the nearest sandwich shop, which, as closing time approaches, will have reduced the price of its egg sandwiches in an effort to sell them before they go off. You should be able to buy one for about £1.20. You dash back to the office and, just as your colleague is about to rifle through your briefcase to see if you've nicked his food again, hand him the new, cheaper sandwich. You have made £1.30 profit. He has still eaten his egg sandwich. There is no loser.

There are ways of making this transaction even more profitable, principally by artificially forcing down the price of egg sandwiches. This is most easily achieved by spreading malevolent rumours about the product to destroy public confidence in it and force panicked selling by the owners. For example, you might pose as a health and safety inspector and pin a notice on the window of the sandwich shop announcing that a massive infestation of cockroaches has been found in the kitchen; or you could waltz in casually for your lunchtime couscous and blithely but loudly ask whether they have got their salmonella problem under control yet; or you could ask your friend who works on the local evening paper to run a huge front-page headline reading "Egg sandwiches cause liver cirrhosis". Sure enough, the price will plummet further, and you should be able to acquire your egg sandwich for free, when the shop throws all its unused food into the bins out the back door. Admittedly, the shop would probably shut down for the foreseeable future, making further such profiteering more difficult logistically, but you will be £2.50 richer, and that is all that counts.

If you removed the human traders from the London Stock Exchange and replaced them with an infinite number of monkeys, would the markets go up or down?

Habib Marwan, 20, juggler, Lowestoft

ACCORDING TO TOP PRIMATE economist Professor Hopton McGonagle, the Monkey Exchange would, from a distance, appear the same as the old-style, pre-computer Stock Exchange – a lot of squawking, scrabbling, face-pulling and genital-grabbing, but not a lot of dignity.

Once initial logistical teething problems had been

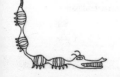

overcome[17] and the monkeys began trading, they would inevitably climb over, play with and hump the exchange's modern computers. Statistically, the resulting untargeted pressing of buttons would likely result in an almost equal amount of buying as selling at all times, thus ensuring greater market stability than the primates' human predecessors have traditionally provided.

From a worldwide perspective, McGonagle, 57, predicts that if the Monkey Exchange began trading on a Monday morning, the global markets would initially respond positively to the sight of London seeming to buy and sell with such frantic energy. However, as the day progressed, the animals' initial enthusiasm would wear off, and many would probably take a snooze, which typically affects world share prices adversely.[18] The end result globally would be the maintenance of the status quo.

Thus, the markets would neither rise nor fall significantly. The monkeys would not produce the

17 In addition to obvious procedural difficulties, such as recruiting, feeding and cleaning up after such a large quantity of creatures, practical problems must be overcome – for example, the Exchange's current Paternoster Square headquarters are of a finite size, so it would have to move to new, infinitely large, premises (which would therefore probably have to be located outside London).

18 Some blame the 'Black Monday' crash of 1987 on new Federal Reserve Chairman Alan Greenspan being seen to have a five-minute nap on his desk following his regular lunchtime game of Musical Chairs.

large profits needed to drive economic growth, nor the large losses which destroy financial stability. However, the damage to local ecosystems around the monkey world from removing so many creatures from their natural environments would be significant, and therefore this is a scheme which should, for the foreseeable future, remain a purely hypothetical one.[19]

It is worth noting that Science, deceitful she-devil that he is, has proven that some brands of monkey do already operate a primitive bartering system. However, by contrast with a human stock exchange, this is based on mutually beneficial co-operation to ensure social wellbeing, rather than hoodwinking others to maximise personal gain. The scientists reluctantly concluded that monkeys would eternally be restricted in their efforts to create a human-style economic system by their more advanced simian ethical compass. This, tragically, will preclude them from buying their way out of poverty, and will therefore stunt their evolution as a species.

Incidentally, the Infinite Monkey theory has been partially proven right by a secret government

---

19 A planned control experiment in which an infinite number of stock market traders were to be put in a monkey sanctuary was cancelled after a computer simulation suggested it would lead to a significant decrease in the number of paying visitors.

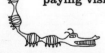

experiment with a very large number of monkeys and other primates, an equally large number of typewriters, and an on-site Shakespeare scholar. The test has been running since 1967 in a giant laboratory beneath Milton Keynes, the new town which was specially constructed to house all the civil servants involved in feeding, cleaning and motivating the menagerie, and in repairing the frequently banana-jammed typewriters.

Although, at time of going to press, the monkeys have not yet generated even one full Shakespeare play, let alone the full caboodle, a pygmy marmoset did on one occasion type the full lyrics to Millie Small's classic 1964 ska-pop hit 'My Boy Lollipop'; while in 1994 a family of stump-tailed macaques wrote the first 18 minutes of a 1995 episode of Australian soap opera 'Neighbours'.[20]

---

20 'Neighbours' script editors have refuted allegations of plagiarism levelled at them by the monkeys' literary agent, and have claimed the identical scripts to be "the kind of coincidence that happens in a big planet like this".

I've heard people on the telly talk about a 'dead cat bounce' without showing the slightest bit of concern for the deceased pet. Who are these people, and what are they talking about?

Antwaan Randle Em, 41, American football
tribute act, Washington

THESE PEOPLE ARE ECONOMIC correspondents, and the 'dead cat bounce' is a brief and slight recovery of a collapsing stock price, which immediately precedes a subsequent corpse-like flopping onto the economic floor.

The dead cat bounce was discovered during the 'Black Monday' crash of October 1987. Wall Street commodities trader Butane K. Cronk Jr, returning home in high dudgeon from a disastrous day's speculating, angrily hurled his Chihuahua out of the window of his downtown 33rd-floor apartment. He then unsuccessfully tried to console his dog-loving wife by remarking wryly how the trajectory of their ex-pet almost exactly mirrored that of some of his shares that afternoon.

Cronk lay awake that night, tossing and turning as he mulled over the day's events. The dog's flight-landing path was close to his stocks' plummet curve, but not precisely the same. With what little money

he had left, he embarked on an extensive programme of animal defenestration to find the creature whose fall and death most accurately mimicked a doomed share price. Two months and several Central Park Zoo banning orders later, he concluded that it was in fact the humble household cat.

Further investigation revealed that an exact parabolic match could be achieved with a recently deceased cat, rather than a living one or an even deader cat already suffering from rigor mortis. Thus, the term 'dead cat bounce' was coined.

Some nose-diving share prices do not bounce at all, but merely hurtle straight into commercial oblivion causing widespread mess on the trading room floor; these are known as 'dead cat splats'. Other stocks are obviously doomed, but decline slowly in value before settling at their final point of worthlessness. These are known as 'unwanted Christmas kittens', after the trajectory of a bag containing four baby tabbies and a brick when dropped into a canal in late January.

Satirical Bulgario-American NBA basketball player LaJarvis Stoichkov once bounced a dead cat all the way up the court at Madison Square Garden, when playing for the Minneapolis Widows against the New York Forks. The 6'12" Stoichkov, who also played for the Albuquerque Albumens, the Wichita Shower Cubicles, the Orlando Orifices, Memphis

Rash and the Boston Skin Grafts in a hall-of-fame career, then slam-dunked the kitty cadaver before ripping off his shirt to reveal a tattoo warning fans of the dangers of short-selling.

'Dead Cat' Bounce was also a 1930s blues singer from Scraping, Michigan, who specialised in songs about share prices. Born McKinley Bounce in 1898, his hits included 'My Baby (Can't Bear The Bear Market)', 'Capitalisation-Weighted Portfolio Blues', 'Boom Boom Boom Bust' and 'Hoochie Coochie Investor'.

Christian capitalists have been known to buy shares of failed companies on the principle that they may do a Jesus bounce – in other words, fall through no fault of their own after being persecuted by opportunistic traders, settle for a couple of days, and then rise again and take their place high in economic heaven. Other traders do not believe this has ever happened to a share price.

Cats are all the rage in economics. How fat does a cat have to be to qualify to be a 'fat cat'?

Anke Messerschmidt, 12, aviation heiress, Berlin

BEING A FAT CAT, or, to give it its medical name, felinocorpulentilism, is a serious psychiatric condition whose severity is often underestimated due to the lampooning of the gutter press.

It is important to remember that fat-cattedness is a state of mind, not a state of income. It causes a chemical imbalance in the soul which can lead to irrational behaviour such as limousine-hiring, cigar-smoking and yacht-owning.

The extent of public and media disgust with fat cats often correlates directly with the ostentatiousness with which the executives in question carry their furry commercial paunches. Some fat cats, however, are so morbidly financially obese that their jelly-like affluence wobbles in nauseating waves of excess, putting people off their food as they contemplate how it is possible to carry so much wealth without collapsing under the sheer weight of it.

FAT CAT FACT BOX

- In some countries, Fat Cat is an official tax band, above higher-rate taxation. Fat Cat income is usually taxed at anything between 0 and 3 per cent.

- Schrödinger's Cat is a paradoxical thought experiment by legendary Austrian physics virtuoso Erwin Schrödinger, in which he claimed that, under the notoriously unjust laws of quantum mechanics, a cat can be simultaneously dead and alive. Schrödinger's Fat Cat is a similar experiment by his economist brother Borscht, who claimed to have proved that a businessman, if he borrows huge amounts of money without the realistic prospect of ever being able to pay it back, can be both rich and poor at the same time.

- The letters 'FC' are used as an abbreviation for Fat Cat, although some claim it is an abbreviation for an altogether less complimentary term.

- Ironically, in evolutionary terms the fat cat is extremely poorly designed. Vulnerable to hostile predators, unable to change direction quickly, and reliant on handouts of milk and sardines, the fat cat would have died out by now had it not been artificially preserved by government-sponsored conservation programmes and tax loopholes.

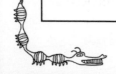

If I ever have a job, the chances are that I'll get bored of it pretty damn quickly. But I quite fancy having a crack at being Chancellor of the Exchequer; it can't be as difficult as it looks on the telly. However, I have never actually governed or chancelled anything. So what should I put on my CV to give myself the best chance of nailing the job?

Taufiq Riswas, 14, pencil-balancing
champion, Karachi

A s much as possible. Talk yourself up, because getting into Number 11 Downing Street is becoming increasingly difficult.

Being Chancellor of the Exchequer is not quite the glamorous job it appears to be on Budget Day, when the Chancellor has only to emerge from his special house on Downing Street carrying the right colour briefcase to attract the flash-bulbs of the world's paparazzi, before being broadcast – live and uninterrupted – to the entire nation for an hour or more, in the kind of unadulterated media exposure of which most celebrities can only dream.

Nevertheless, it remains one of the toughest jobs to get – there is only one such position in the country, and historically almost all successful candidates have been able to boast a successful or prominent career in politics. So you will have to spruce up your CV even more than you usually do for job applications to even stand a chance.

Successful CVs, like history documentaries, are traditionally a winning mixture of actual fact, enhanced fact, and plausible lie.[21] When going for the Chancellor job, it is important that your lies are not too outlandish. If you make yourself appear too successful, your interviewers (i.e. the Prime Minister, his wife or wives, and some of their best friends) will think you overqualified for the job, and wonder why you are not pursuing a more lucrative and influential career in the private sector.

Therefore you should claim that you helped raise £50 for your local hedgehog sanctuary by organising a fake Blue Peter bring-and-buy sale, but not boast that you transformed your local corner shop into the world's third most profitable retail brand with an annual turnover of £943 million. Recent evidence suggests that it is also essential that you declare yourself to be both Scottish and dour.

Should you make it through to the interview stage, you must strike the optimum balance between mid-level competence, moral elasticity,

---

21 Recent Department for Work and Pensions research revealed that the average British job applicant's CV is 43% true.

74

and short-term expediency. You must also display a total immunity to giggling. A Chancellor must never display any outward signs of humour whilst in office – such facial slips could cause panic in the money markets. Your interviewers will therefore test your ability to withstand common giggle provokers. One of them may break wind at an audible-but-unobtrusive volume or, deliberately but with a straight face, repeatedly refer to the French stock market index – the CAC – before starting to abbreviate all references to Chambers of Commerce to 'COC's.

Such tests are part of the everyday trial of being Chancellor – you must be able to resist the rising surge of the snigger. This is arguably the second most important quality in a Chancellor, after the ability to take credit for prevailing global trends during good times, and to deflect blame onto the world in general when things turn bad.

I think I've been really good this year. I deserve an annual bonus. How do I calculate how much to give myself?

Des Lyneham, 55, ice cream vendor, Cromer

THE CRISIS HAS TAUGHT us that, no matter how bad business has been, everyone deserves a bonus. Alan H. Fishman joined Washington Mutual, one of America's biggest banks, on 8 September 2008. Three weeks and a record-breaking bankruptcy later, Fishman was $19 million richer, courtesy of a $7.5 million signing-on fee, an $11.6 million cash severance, and $4 he won on the office fruit machine before moon-walking out of the building and high-fiving himself so hard that he dislocated both wrists. And Petruvia Hujgjoëns, the Chief Financial Officer of the Johnny Rep Memorial Aquarium in Holland, was given three dead basking sharks as a redundancy pay-off when the business went bust. This followed her reduction of the water budget to nil in order to pay for a new blast-proof swivel chair and space-travel-enabled filing cabinet for her office.

In the finance sector, the annual bonus is calculated from a complex series of interconnecting variables, ranging from snappiness of suit, garishness of tie, and pointitude of shoe, to number

of small businesses destroyed, quantity of third-world children indirectly starved, and number of puffs of cigar smoke blown in waitresses' eyes during business lunches in titty bars with dubious Russian billionaires.

For high-ranking executives, bonuses should be big enough to amaze and appal the watching world, but small enough not to bankrupt the entire company.[22] For maximum satisfaction, any bonus over £250,000 should be presented as a suitcase full of used £10 notes, handed over by a large Eastern European or Colombian man in sunglasses, while a colleague in an overcoat brandishes a gun smiles and nods cockishly.

Though such rewards are beyond the reach, comprehension and calculators of most ordinary people, there is no reason to miss out on the Age Of The Ludicrous Pay-Off: you simply need to declare yourself self-employed, and then award yourself an extravagantly gargantuan Christmas bonus. For example, begin trading on December 23 as a self-employed home illuminations consultant. Give yourself a nice little festive perk of £1.2 million, as a performance-related reward for successfully replacing the worthy but dingy 15-watt energy saving lightbulb in your kitchen with a proper

---

22 The first part of this has been easily achieved. The second has proved more difficult.

old-fashioned 100-watt job. You deserve it – the extra visibility could easily prevent you slicing a finger off while chopping a cucumber.

Admittedly, since you will be paying yourself the money, this sum will have no actual effect on your net overall earnings. However, the positive psychological impact on you could be immense. It will give you, as your own employee, a significant morale boost knowing that your employer (you) prizes you so highly. It will also make you, as your own employer, feel like Captain Billy Big-Shot, ostentatiously chucking money around like a 1980s film star at the opening of an upmarket burger joint. Both you and you will begin to think that you truly belong in the high-rolling world of 21st-century finance.

You will also come to understand an important lesson – that how much someone earns and how much someone is paid are often two wildly differing figures, as demonstrated by areas of life such as business, politics, twenty-over cricket matches and nursing.

In the light of the Credit Crunch, does the result of the Cold War still stand?

Blind Lemon Haämäpajaäminen, 82,
Finnish blues singer, Helsinki

T HE RESULT DOES STAND, despite recent nationalisations of banks: Capitalism beat Communism. If you are still in doubt, go to Berlin, climb over a wall, and see whether or not you get shot. However, the margin of victory is being reassessed, and if it ever goes to a second leg, it is still anyone's.

The Crunch has not shown Capitalism at its sparkling, free-market best. Its inherent flaws, such as human nature, have been shown up. Were Lenin alive today, however, he would not be punching the lid of his coffin in celebration just yet – the British government may have bought out Northern Rock, but they have stopped short of driving tanks through Trafalgar Square and dispatching poets to a labour camp in Cornwall. Given the rapid collapse of the Eastern bloc in the late 20th century, and the embarrassing humiliations of Western banking in the 21st, the Capitalism vs. Communism contest is starting to look like one of those matches which will be remembered not for the final score but for both sides disgracing themselves – the political equivalent of Chile versus Italy in the 1962 football World Cup, a game known as 'The Battle Of Santiago'.

This explosion of sporting vitriol and violence was the closest international football has ever come to recreating an authentic medieval war. It had everything that Ultimate Fighting Championship fans could possibly want in a game of football apart from a cage, and the official match ball was later quoted as saying: "I honestly don't know what I was doing on the pitch."

And the result of the match? No-one knows. All that was left were the indelible mental images of an Italian man booting a Chilean man in the head and a Chilean man thwacking an Italian man on the nose, and a lingering sense of pointless carnage and everyone having let themselves down. Football was the loser. It was like the Cold War, but with actual violence instead of empty threats. Point proven.

Judging by the way the FTSE Index has been going, buying shares nowadays is like an orange – completely pointless.[23] Is there

---

23 This joke is referring to the shape of the orange, not its worth as an object. The orange is round, and therefore has no physical point. As a fruit, it is both tasty and nutritious, and makes outstanding juice, so without question it has a

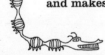

any good reason to own shares any more?

Gordon Roadstand, 72, retired stadium critic, Gillingham

POSSIBLY, BUT IT IS a risky business, and not one you should enter for financial gain. The skittishly temperamental stock markets have been going up and down like the proverbial fiddler's elbow – and this particular fiddler is really letting it rip on an unusually vigorous violin version of a throbbing nightclub dance anthem, whilst

---

point in the 'purpose' sense of the word. This joke is therefore potentially confusing, as well as insulting to orange-lovers. It might have worked better with 'a snooker ball' in place of 'an orange'; the snooker ball is a perfectly spherical object, whereas some oranges taper towards their top end. However, since snooker is a point-based game in which each ball has a potential numerical value, it too could confuse a reader in the context of this joke. Any round object may suffer similar problems, due to the semantic ambiguity of the word 'pointless'. Hence for the joke to work to its optimum level, the object being compared to the buying of shares must be pointless both in its physical form and in its practical futility. Possible things for share-buying to be as pointless as include: 'a non-existent railway junction', 'a steamrollered mole on the A303', 'a compass made of salt on a rainy day', 'a cancelled table tennis match', or (to retain the innate humour of the word 'orange') 'a sword shaped like an orange'. Football supporters may wish to further exploit the sporting connotations of 'pointless' by adding, as a coda to any of the above lines, 'which plays for **X**', where **X** is a football team currently struggling at the bottom of a league table. This footnote, ironically, is also pointless (notwithstanding a further meaning of the word 'point', i.e. 'a mark of punctuation').

simultaneously inflating a punctured football with a hand pump, repeatedly punching a sleeping beggar, and gradually leaning down to pick up a chocolate bonbon off the floor. All in all, that is a lot of elbow, not a lot of end product, an overall downward trend, and a general feeling of confusion and futility. Welcome to 21st-century economics.

Therefore, if you want to invest financially in company shares, you should do so for the same reason that people invest emotionally in sports teams – to feel involved in a business. Share-owning also makes watching 24-hour rolling business news channels far more exciting.

Furthermore, it is more important than ever that you research the background of any company whose shares you are contemplating buying. The High Court recently threw out a compensation claim brought by an investor who purchased £5,000 of shares in the Titanic from a door-to-door stockbroker. The latter gave the deal an impressive sales pitch, making it seem an unmissable investment opportunity – a top-of-the-range ocean liner with a maximum speed of 23 knots, kitted out in a charming retro early 20th-century style, and with tenacious musicians. The Court ruled that it was the investor's responsibility to have found out that the ship had sunk 95 years previously.

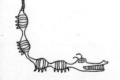

I like sport. In fact, I need sport – it helps me distract myself from the harsh realities of reality. Will the Credit Crunch spoil sport just like it has ruined so many of my other hobbies, like cheering for the FTSE Index, overpaying wildly for houses, and having a job?

Kelly Stonehenge, 46, lipstick consultant,
Glasgow

SPORT HAS JUMPED ONTO the big business bandwagon with characteristic athleticism. However, in doing so, it has embraced debt as if debt had just scored a spectacular last-minute 25-yard volley to win the World Cup. This leaves it as vulnerable to these turbulent times as anything else that has brainlessly thrown millions of pounds at the golden goose in an effort to make it feel more golden and thus lay bigger and more golden eggs.

Football, for example, has been paying its players 20 times more money in an effort to convince them subliminally that they are 20 per cent better at football. This money does not grow on trees. It grows on TV contracts. And TV contracts do not grow on trees.

The whole spangly anti-competitive edifice is ultimately dependent on supporters continuing to sacrifice their money on the altar of escapist fantasy. And while this has hitherto proved a reliable source of income, it is at least theoretically possible that football fans may begin to analyse their outgoings of money and time, and decide that, adorable though their clubs may be, they do actually also like their families and children a bit, and are prepared to invest financially and temporally in them too.

So sport is at risk. However, it is imperative for the psychological wellbeing of the human race as a species that sport remains and even enhances its current status of public prominence and popularity.

Such is the gloom surrounding the planet at present that the demand for high-quality distractions such as sport will continue to grow, and governments and business have a duty to their fellow humans to give them the maximum number of things to obsess about other than the various man-made catastrophes looming in the wing-mirror like an especially cocksure drunken lorry driver.

Sport is by far the most effective of these. It was invented specifically to distract humanity from the crushing realisation of inevitable suffering.

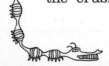

The ancient Greeks developed the Olympic games when they realised that watching naked men run around, wrestle and throw stuff was more entertaining than sitting at home waiting to die prematurely. The Romans later gave their people the gladiatorial arena to deflect public attention from their emperors chatting up farm animals. And golf was invented to give businessmen the opportunity not to speak to their wives – a win-win solution for both sides.

Not only can sport detach our brains from matters of concern, but it can also engender unsurpassable levels of national pride to puncture the prevailing feel-bad factor of economic gloom.[24] The Beijing Olympics, for example, proved that we will willingly weep tears of salty pride when someone we have never met wins an event we had never heard of in a place several thousand miles away that we don't like to think too carefully about.

Such is the strength of the illogically optimistic emotions engendered by sporting glory, that it

---

24 The power of sporting distractivity reached its zenith during the Cold War. Eastern European regimes formulated a clever mathematical equation in which the number of the human rights abuses the state could get away with rose in direct proportion to the number of Olympic medals won. They duly began pumping their sportsmen so full of steroids that their male athletes were soon all but unbeatable in both men's and women's events.

makes rock-solid economic sense for the British government to purchase success at whatever price necessary. And as the value of money goes down, so the value of sporting glory goes up – winning a bronze medal in three-day eventing has been proven scientifically to have to same impact on national morale as giving every single person in the country £4.30 in cash, or a free pint of beer and packet of nuts.

Little of our once great manufacturing sector remains outside of museums, and our much-vaunted financial sector now spends most of its time shuffling awkwardly next to the coffee machine, mumbling "oops". Yet our harvest of Olympic medals has become increasingly bounteous in recent years. The only conclusion to draw is that the time has come for Britain to devote its time, resources and energies exclusively to the acquisition of sporting medals and trophies. The streets of Britain would soon be inundated with a thousand Rebecca Adlingtons, countless Chris Hoys and infinite Phil 'The Power' Taylors. Life will become one unending celebration of our national superiority over other countries which have prioritised other areas of life.

It is not only future achievements that should be targeted, however. Everything has its price, and

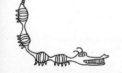

Britain remains a relative economic powerhouse. It should use what is left of its withering financial muscle to buy historic triumphs from other, poorer nations. The whopping boost to national morale of the government purchasing Brazil's five World Cup triumphs would be incalculable. The trophies could be split roughly pro rata through the UK – 1958, 1962 and 2002 to be given to England, 1994 to be won jointly by Wales and Northern Ireland, and the glorious 1970 tournament to be awarded to Scotland, who will be able to claim to have defeated Italy 4-1 in the final, with the brilliant Jim Baxter at the heart of a breathtaking display of attacking football.

My friend doesn't like sport. Is there anything the government can do to keep him happy?

Bukis Andsahd, 21, toy describer, Manchester

FIRSTLY, YOUR FRIEND IS wrong. Secondly, yes, there is: space travel.

The Cold War taught us many things, principally that the world will never be truly safe until every individual is armed with his or her own personal nuclear deterrent, thus achieving a worldwide equilibrium of threat. Amongst its other lessons[25] was that firing people, animals and things into space entertains people far more effectively than nuclear brinksmanship.

A new space race is exactly what the world needs at the moment. The government should announce plans to fire a dog (or, to pacify the animal rights lobby, a person in a dog outfit) at Mars by the year 2020. That is the kind of scheme to which people can relate. Vague environmental targets will have no-one glued to their television screens waiting to hear the pre-scripted historic bark as the rocket touches down.

Record-breaking is another, cheaper method of injecting pride into the national veins. Recent examples of attention-distracting, patriotism-inflating achievements by nations experiencing difficulties include: the world's largest poncho (Columbia – ongoing scuffles with FARC rebels,

---

25 Further Cold War lessons include:

- Do not, under any circumstances, no matter how tempting, sell large-scale ballistic weapons to any person or persons who have a 50-metre-high portrait of themselves somewhere in their capital city. They clearly lack the humility to be trusted with them.

- If you stick a big wall through the middle of the city, people on at least one – possibly both – sides of that wall will become increasingly annoyed (a finding that is in the process of being corroborated in the Middle East).

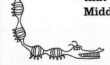

illegal drug trade); the world's largest ostrich sandwich (Iran – bickering with USA, economic problems, allegations of human rights abuses); and the world's largest pumpkin (USA – bickering with Iran, economic problems, allegations of human rights eccentricities).

World records the British government should consider acquiring to further boost national pride are: bendiest pencil, fattest snake, tallest post box, most voluminous bra, loudest klaxon, hottest burrito (temperature and chilli), longest delay, shortest bus, most foreheads simultaneously slapped,[26] most flags in car windows,[27] bandiest gait, grumpiest ticket collector, and most flamboyantly-dressed traffic warden. Any of these would make our internal Union Jacks flutter that little bit more proudly in our tummies.

26 This may be out of Britain's reach. The record is currently 150 million, achieved by the USA on 8 November 2000, the morning after the Presidential election.

27 A record Britain already holds by some margin, and should increase if more than one part of the nation qualifies for the 2010 World Cup.

There are more and more people in this world, and they're staying not dead longer and longer. Given the widespread problems with pension funds and the general decay of the world's economic system, is human life still economically viable?

Chaimie Ar-Ivah, 33, window analyst, Tel Aviv

THIS IS THE PROVERBIAL Elephant In The Room, and she's knocking tea-cups over with her trunk, stealing people's buns, sitting on pot plants, and generally making an oversized nuisance of herself. The fact is that almost all of the world's social and economic problems have been caused by people, and a stable, sustainable economy may not be possible with human involvement.

Human life is riddled with inefficiencies: childhood, for example, and retirement, to name but two of the many unproductive phases of existence. In Britain by 2040, the average 90-year-old codger will have spent a pitiful 9.5 per cent of his life doing anything economically productive [see diagram opposite]. It is little wonder the world has turned out to owe itself so much money.

If the planet wishes to avoid further economic catastrophes in future, it must radically restructure the financial lives of its inhabitants. And the

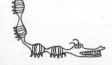

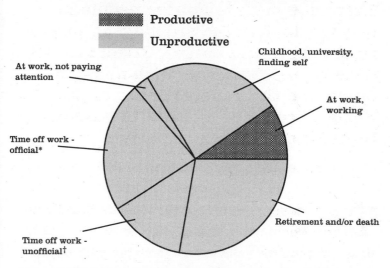

* i.e. weekends, holidays, lunchtime, smoking, evenings, night-time etc
† i.e. sickies, afternoon snoozes, lavatory breaks, general time wasting, office small talk, marriage, child-bearing, child-rearing, hangovers, world cups, crosswords, funerals, surgery, religious worship, etc.

backbone of its future workforce must be children and pensioners – the population groups who have largely dragged it down thus far.[28]

In the unarguable words of George Bernard Shaw, "youth is wasted on the young". They have little desire to be educated, and spend much of their time wishing they were adults – who, by contrast, spend most of their time wishing they were still children, and the rest of it thinking about sport,

---

28 The Confederation of World Industry officially demarcates human beings into three age groups for economic assessment purposes: children as JUBs (juvenile unproductivity burdens); working-age adults as NASGUs (non-aged supervisable grown-ups); and the retired as PDCs (pre-death corpses).

television, and illicit recreational or procreational activities. Adults therefore constitute an extremely inefficient workforce, but, as the Victorians and major clothing manufacturers realised, children can be easily coaxed to work more productively for much less money.

Furthermore, retirement is wasted on the old. They are often too physically and mentally exhausted from a lifetime of work and disappointments to fully appreciate the incredible leisure opportunities that pensioner status offers. Also, as a species, the elderly constantly complain about having nothing to do, and will therefore do whatever is put in front of them. As a lifestyle choice, it makes perfect sense for them to slide gently into the inescapable chasm of annihilation whilst performing valuable manual labour which benefits society as a whole.

Accordingly, in these uniquely desperate financial times, the accepted pattern of human life should be restructured as follows:

Ages 0-3: Infancy. No change. Evolution has left humanity burdened with these years of compulsory redundancy.

Ages 4-13: Manual work. Scientifically, the most controllable age.

Ages 13-18: Clerical and financial work. Tedium controls hormones.

Ages 18-30: Retirement. Should be used for fun, travel, memoir-writing, and any necessary child-rearing (another inbuilt inefficiency imposed upon us by Mother Nature).

Ages 31-40: Education. The best age for it – learning will be more valued.

Ages 41-50: Management. Some of the wisdom of experience, warmed by the final smouldering embers of the vigour of youth.

Ages 51-60: Agriculture. Many people take up gardening in their sixth decade. They might as well garden for a reason.

Ages 61-death: Manual/unskilled work. The security of employment, the comfort of repetition, the eradication of reasons to live too long.

Nevertheless, even this streamlined life path may not be enough for the human race to survive the current economic turn-down. Unemployment is set to become an increasingly irritable albatross around the economy's neck. Recent events also suggest that the financial services industry would be more effective if left completely unstaffed. And many other jobs can now be done electronically – even greetings card messages can be generated entirely by a computer programmed to predict the emotions felt on a birthday, religious festival, court appearance or divorce, and encapsulate them in a four-line rhyme.

As things currently stand, therefore, the continuation of the human race may prove to be financially ruinous. Extinction is probably in the greater economic interest of the species.

How high can the Credit Crunch reach in the League Table of History's Greatest Economic Catastrophes?

Manueda Koch-Blaczt, 53,
sports clairvoyant, Vienna

QUITE HIGH – IF it keeps up its early momentum it could be looking at a podium finish. However, the gold medal will almost certainly remain out of reach, because despite the heroic efforts of modern day bankers and traders, nothing will ever knock Tulip Mania off the top of the economic idiocy tree.

Tulip Mania was not, as is popularly thought, an overpromoted flower show at Wembley Arena aiming to get teenagers interested in gardening again. It was a 17th century Dutch financial bubble brought about by a rabid enthusiasm for tulips. The pointy-leafed flower was a relatively new phenomenon in Europe, and in the words of Höögenhilds van der Kleepstraäten, Holland's top celebrity gardener at the time, it "beat the carpels off the daffodil, and makes the petunia look like

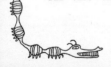

the flaccid waste of flowerpot space we always suspected it to be."

In a continent whose only other hobbies at the time were Catholic-burning and dying of bubonic plague, the tulip rapidly became hugely popular, and the price of its bulbs consequently rose to stratospheric heights. A tulip futures market sprang up, and people from all three major social groups – men, women and old people – risked their entire livelihoods on tulips, in the apparently safe assumption that tulips would always be the most popular form of mass entertainment humanity could possibly devise.[29]

Tulip bulbs became huge celebrities, the premiership footballers of their day – one bulb, which had just been transferred to one of the big tulip growers for 4,000 florins,[30] was seen out on a date with a famous model who had appeared topless

---

29 This may seem quaintly outdated to us now, but it should be remembered that this was still some time before the development of telephone voting.

30 Around £28.3 million in today's money, if wrongly calculated. Under the terms of the transfer deal, the bulb also received a per-petal bonus and exclusive control on its image rights. The leading tabloid newspaper at the time, De Zon, as fixated on celebrity as its modern counterparts, responded with the headline: 'Flor blimey! Tu must be joking.'
   Other flowers' values also rose: '£1,000 a bulb – I-ris I had a few of them!' (Sword Weekly, 1639), 'Rhodo-what-dron?' (The Royalist, 1638), 'Gladiolus – but not so glad-I-owe-£20,000 for it!' (The Sunday Sport, 1640), and '£50,000 for a flower? Y-orchid-ing me!' (Daily Rat, 1643).

in several Rubens paintings. The young Rembrandt, in between painting his own face and doing hidden-easel pictures of women having baths for specialist voyeur art galleries, commanded huge fees just for drawing the outline of a tulip in crayon, and then getting one of his pupils to colour it in. A man was apparently even jailed for accidentally eating a tulip bulb which he mistook for an onion, in perhaps one of most unlucky judicial sentences since Jesus was banged to rights on a charge of being Messianic In Charge Of A Donkey.

However, humankind was about to discover for the first time that the price of tulip bulbs could go down as well as up. Tulip speculators had been buying bulbs with the intention of selling them on for a profit. Inevitably, one day, someone near Amsterdam said: "How much? For a ****ing flower? No thanks, mate." Confidence in the tulip collapsed, prices plummeted like a forgetful parachutist, and people were left with a lot of flowers and not a lot of money. The Netherlandian economy has never recovered[31] – indeed, some blame the lingering after-effects of the tulip crash

---

31 It should perhaps be pointed out that some historians believe Tulip Mania to have been exaggerated by a 19th-century historian with a book to sell, and that market fluctuations were not as extreme as reported, but were more influenced by curious governmental regulation than actual mania for tulips. However, this would be a significantly less good story, and can therefore be discounted for journalistic purposes.

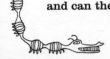

for the Dutch football team's defeat in successive World Cup finals in the 1970s.

To give the episode some context, however, it should be remembered that the 17th century was an especially stupid one, marked by some of the battiest behaviour in human history. In fact, a panel of experts from History Today magazine recently voted the year 1626 one of the three most imbecilic years of all time. In this single, silly year:

- Top-ranking Flemish chemist Jan Baptista van Helmont blotted his otherwise impressive scientific copybook by proposing that diseases are caused by alien beings called "archaea". Big Jan also conducted an experiment in which he claimed to have turned wheat into live mice by leaving it an open jar with some dirty underwear. Having set up the wheat and pants, he scooted off for three weeks, and when he returned, the wheat had disappeared and the rodents had moved in. The man was a certified genius. Less fortunately, he also disproved the theory that if you stand on your head for twenty minutes a day, you will never die.

- Ace philosopher and all-round whizz-kid Francis Bacon died after shoving snow up a hen's arse. His attempts to pioneer frozen chicken caused him to catch a fatal chill. He was clearly an inventive and unsqueamish man, but also, equally clearly, a bit of an idiot.

- The inhabitants of Manhattan sold their island to Dutch chancer Peter Minuit for twenty quid and some buttons. It is now worth at least sixty times as much.

Jesus was known to throw the odd strop about greedy traders. He once went ballistic at some local businessmen who had set up a bureau de change in his favourite temple, and gave the dove-sellers a piece of his holy mind as well. What would the former magician and raconteur think of recent events?

Sausage McGraw, 62, private investigator,
Streatham

ACCORDING TO A LEAKED rumour from the Archbishop of Canterbury's vestry, sources close to Jesus suggest that he is "privately fuming" at the state of the world's financial system, and "not at all chuffed" with the behaviour of America in particular, home to so many of his most ardent fans.[32]

The former convict and beard enthusiast is also said to be "sick and tired" at his teachings being misinterpreted, and sometimes does not know "why [he] bothered if this was all that people were going to make of it".

In one of his more surreal moments, Jesus once said: "It is easier for a camel to pass through the eye of a needle than for a rich man to enter the Kingdom of God." These words have been pounced upon by evangelical Christian capitalists, who claim that:

(a) the international failure to solve world poverty, which some blame on the iniquities of globalisation, merely shows the rich nations and corporations of the world selflessly helping to fast-track the world's poor through Heaven's notoriously restrictive immigration policy; and

(b) only the financial muscle and entrepreneurial spirit of capitalism can enable us to manufacture either giant needles with just-above-camel-sized

---

32 In 2008 the USA retained its trophies for World's Biggest Capitalist and World's Most Christian Nation – two titles that few thought would ever be unified. Prominent American television star Prebell Chicken Jr, the in-house socialist for atheist cable channel No God TV, described winning these two competitions as "like being really good at both life-saving and murder, or like justifying cannibalism by claiming to be a really good cook."

eyes, or an efficient industrial camel mincer that can create a camel sausage with a 0.5mm diameter, threadable through all standard household embroidery needles.

It has long been a tradition in the wealthier nations of the world to outsource our biggest problems to the world's poor. Will we be able to pull that off this time?

Ferdinand Hildebrand, 76, DIY store advertising jingle composer, Beverley Hills

THE EARLY SIGNS ARE not good. Though the poor will undoubtedly share in our misfortune, disappointingly we will not be able to outsource all of the problems to them in the traditional manner. It is even possible that the poor, if they are prepared to put enough money into it, could actually take advantage of the wealthier nations' current troubles.

One of the great concerns of the current crisis has been that, while the poor may lose what little they had, the middle and upper classes of the world could lose far more of what they didn't have. So the net result will in fact be far worse for the well-off than the needy. If anything, it is the poor who have least to lose. They don't know how fortunate they are.[33]

We have seen the same pattern in the world food crisis. It has affected billions of people from all walks of life around the world in different ways: some people are being forced to pay slightly more for their groceries; others, for example, are having to starve to death. It has been a lifestyle shift for everyone. In Britain, the average family food bill has risen by around £15 – without the succour of having free tasty snacks airdropped on us like the lucky Africans do.

There have even been food riots around the world – in Haiti, the Philippines and elsewhere, people protested about the scarcity and rising price of rice, for example. This may surprise British consumers, who, in recent market research, mostly claimed that they find rice "OK, but a bit dull" as a food, and could "quite easily" live without it. Clearly the people of Haiti and the Philippines are fussier eaters than we are.

All in all, however, the world's poor are already shaping up to have another bad millennium. That

---

33 Alfred Lord Tennyson may have disagreed. In 1850, the Poet Laureate received a £10,000 advance from his publisher for a new limerick about a young lady named Jill. That evening, he blew the lot during a boozy night out at the greyhounds with fellow poetry star Robert Browning. Tennyson then wrote: "'Tis better to have earned and lost than never to have earned at all."

would make it nine bad millennia in a row for the poor, which is beginning to look like a habit. The problem is that the poor, as a race, continue to repeat the same mistakes year after year, generation after generation, epoch after epoch. They consistently leave themselves vulnerable to dangerous predators such as famine, drought, other natural disasters, the harsh expediencies of global capitalism, Western indifference and/or imperialism (the two often dancing hand-in-hand like the illicit lovers they are), and crocodiles.

Poverty being relative,[34] the financial collapses in the richer parts of the world have in fact done more to reduce comparative poverty than a million awareness wristbands ever could.

---

34 A child in a playground with £50 is rich. A man in a Rolls Royce showroom with £50 is not rich.

The economy has been collapsing like a Victorian lady at the sight of a gentleman's danglers. What can we, as individual consumers, do to help Britain recover?

Aston Lumpsbury, 38, soul physiotherapist,
Dorking

THE ECONOMY NEEDS MONEY – as famous music hall act Fantabulous Fiscal Freddie sang in the 1890s: "An economy without money/ Quite pointless it would be, Mrs Winch,/ Like badminton with no gravity./ As unenticing as some bread/ On which a rat has bled, Mrs Winch,/ And as ineffective as a dog without a head./ Heigh ho, Mrs Winch, heigh ho I say,/ I'm solvent – and that's what makes me gay. Toodle pip."

So we all have a solemn, patriotic duty at this time of financial crisis to give it that money, to save the British economy in its hour of need by continuing to spend our hard-earned cash on the proverbial High Street.[35]

This is our generation's Dunkerque. When your grandchildren sit on your kneecaps in years to come and ask you, "Granny and/or Granddad, what

---

35 Easy-earned or unearned cash has, interestingly, exactly the same effect on the economy as hard-earned cash. Economics is therefore less enamoured of telling families how hard-working they are than politics is.

did you do in the Credit Crunch?", do you want to have to shuffle awkwardly, point out of the window at a non-existent chaffinch, cough nervously, and start singing a pretend nursery rhyme about squirrels to distract them?

Or do you want to stand up, turn to salute the silver-plated Alistair Darling maquette on your mantelpiece, look them square in their tiny little faces, and bark proudly: "Dennis and/or Petula, my boy and/or girl, I bought a 60-inch plasma-screen TV. And a 58-inch plasma screen TV. For emergencies. I didn't lie down and let credit crunch me. I put my borrowed financial dentures back in, and crunched credit back. I was a hero."

Is that wise? Didn't excessive spending land us in this scalding tank of economic porridge in the first place?

Danika Bocskics, 40, traffic jam assessor, London

YES, BUT GOVERNMENTS HAVE responded by encouraging more such spending, offering inducements such as tax rebates and interest rate cuts. Celebrity Italian economiste and glamour model La Soldícciona explained in an interview with Nuts magazine: "When you have spent your way into trouble, you have spend your way out of trouble. Similarly, if you've driven your car into a lion enclosure, you don't blame the car, abandon it, and try to jump over the fence. No no. You stay in the car, you rev it up more aggressively, you try to scare the lions with a wheelspin, and drive out through the fence. Don't worry, someone else will fix the fence. It's fine."

On the advice of a friend, I took my life savings away from the risk-heavy environment of the bank and invested them all in porcelain dogs, reasoning that while fashions may come and go, people will always need porcelain dogs. Is anything else still a safe investment now?

Janet Mohammed-Perkins, 39, chairperson,
Anglo-Saudi Dating Agency

N o. Putting money in a bank account and leaving it there had hitherto been assumed to be the safest way of not losing that money. However, recent events have shown that it was in fact tantamount to betting on a thousand-to-one-on favourite in the 2.40 at Market Rasen. Even if the horse wins, you won't win much; and there is an increasingly large risk that the nag in question will (a) pull up lame, (b) be knobbled by a dodgy betting syndicate, or (c) be distracted by a rival horse falling over unexpectedly, lose confidence, and jump into an ice cream van.

There is no means of saving that can be guaranteed to be risk-free. The famous circus critic Hubert Fluke,[36] a renowned tightwad, stored all his cash under his bedroom floorboards for safekeeping. However, he was so concerned about potential burglaries that whenever he left his house, he took the money and the floorboards with him. When housebound and bed-ridden in later life, and seeking the additional financial security that would soon be provided for him by death, he nailed extra layers of floorboards on top of the original floorboards, until eventually it became physically impossible to enter or leave the room. He died aged 98, penniless and peckish, in a house fire. His final thought was one of relief that his money worries were at last at an end, and he thoroughly enjoyed the last few blazing seconds of his life. Ironically, while the

36 Fluke was chief circus correspondent for The Times from 1926 until 1971, and thus one of the most influential journalists of the 20th century. He famously described the 1938 touring Moscow State Circus as "an elongated monotony of vapid bestial subjugation, punctuated only by morsels of quarter-baked clowning that were at best derivative to the point of tedious burlesque, and at worst a crime against all humanity. One star."

paper banknotes added to the ferocity of the blaze, the metal coins melted and formed a cast around his body, preserving his parting smile for eternity.

Other than figurines,[37] perhaps the safest long-term investments are:

- romancing, seducing and marrying an heir or heiress to a multi-billion pound family fortune;
- becoming a monk or nun;
- giving birth to a daughter, and hot-housing her from the age of three months to become a professional tennis player;[38]
- shares in a greetings card firm that specialises in recession-based slogans such as "I am so sorry for your job loss", "Merry redundancy", and "Many happy repossessions";
- a bet that, at some point in the next 50 years, the financial markets will forget this current crisis ever happened, get greedy, and repeat exactly the same mistakes, step by irresponsible step; and

---

37 Annual sales of porcelain animals and other decorative household statuettes, when calculated on a figurines sold per 1,000 population basis, have remained constant to within a 1.5% margin since the first known figurine was created around 30,000BC.

38 Focus on developing a two-handed backhand, infinite patience, a fear of proximity to nets, and a lack of imagination.

- historical artefacts that you may one day be able to sell to the Museum Of Financial Folly, which will be (or at least ought to be) set up to warn future generations of the pitfalls of money. Recent economics-related artefacts sold at auction include Queen Victoria's last credit card, on which she left the first three instalments for the Boer War unpaid on her death, and Neville Chamberlain's Mastercard, the bill for which shows that he paid a certain Mr A. Hitler 85,000 Czechoslovak corunas for a single autographed piece of paper. Big Neville was properly hoodwinked, and little Adolf had filched himself some spending money for his forthcoming holiday.

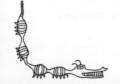

I've got a few financial problems that need sorting out. Let's put it this way – if I don't sort them out, a debt-collection agency is going to come round next week and nail my nadgers to the kitchen floor. The government is only too willing to dish out health and safety advice to me on how to clean a dustbin without falling into it, how to drive without crashing fatally, and how to smoke without killing your work colleagues, but can't they give me some useful advice on dealing with my debt?

Alana Greenspan, 22, burlesque economist, Soho

THEY COULD, AND PROBABLY have, but no-one will take any notice. Most people have become so disillusioned with Westminster politics[39] that they are increasingly taking any government advice not only with an enormous pinch of salt, but also with a giant wedge of lemon, before slamming the advice back so fast they can't even taste it, then waking up at 5 o'clock in the morning in the middle of a roundabout with a vague recollection of the

---

39 The extent of public disillusionment with party politics is proven by the fact that there are more suicides during party conference season than during the rest of the year put together. This is a lie, but the point stands.

government having told them to do something, and vowing to themselves never to listen to a politician ever, ever again.

Furthermore, when it comes to debt, the government has to operate on a "Do As I Say, Not Do As I Do" basis (and given what governments habitually do, this is wise advice, for which politicians receive insufficient credit). In the current financial climate, any government statement urging people to be careful with their money and save for the future will come across as indigestibly rich from an organisation that is clocking up record levels of borrowing whilst splurging its pocket money comfort-buying Olympic Gameses.

The situation is even more extreme in the USA, whose national debt recently smashed through the magical $10 trillion barrier.[40] When George Washington slapped one War Of Independence on his nation's credit card in 1791 for a now-bargain price of $75 million, he surely could not have dreamt that his inspirational "Fight Today, Pay Tomorrow" scheme would still be so strongly pursued in the early 21st century.

---

40 This means that, if all of America's creditors called their debts in simultaneously, demanding objects or people to the value of their debt, and independent valuers adjudged each individual American to be worth an average of $34,000, there would be no-one left in the USA.

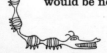

It's all very well me cutting back on my expenditure, but what's the point if the government keeps spending money like it's going out of fashion? Can't they economise too?

Scurf McGinty, 19, dancer, Blackpool

IT WOULD BE DIFFICULT. In essence, the art of modern democratic government is to spend vast amounts of money on being seen to be doing stuff, financed by cutting back spending on actually doing anything. Therefore, governments will not – perhaps cannot – economise significantly, because the less they spend, the less they can be appear to be doing, and therefore the less reason they have to exist.

Another factor is that, regardless of how little or much the government actually spends, many of us will always complain about them wasting taxpayers' money on unnecessary luxuries, such as dialysis machines for other people's kidneys when ours work fine, education for other people's children when ours have already left school, and wars for democracy when we don't even vote.

Furthermore, there are few areas of public life which have not already felt the icy blade of budgetary expedience trembling on their unprotectable necks. In recent decades, it has been decided that perks of everyday existence – such as transport, dentistry, the teaching of languages, dignity for the over-75s, jobs in rural areas, working military equipment, and funding for minor royals – are simply unaffordable in this era of responsible public spending. But further savings could be scrimped in certain costly areas of government expenditure, including:

- NHS surgeons to be paid on a per-save basis.
- Teachers to be paid nothing at point of delivery, but to be remunerated 25 years in the future, based on an independent assessment of how successful their pupils have been since leaving school.
- Civil liberties to be significantly cut back. In general, they damage economic productivity by unnaturally shortening the working day and precluding the motivational use of big sticks; they clog up the judicial system, by requiring such impediments as juries, lawyers for defendants, and proof; and they force us to waste considerable amounts of public money on things like a non-secret police force, the staging and publicising of elections in which millions of people refuse to participate, and actually counting the votes of those that do take part. In sum, civil liberties cost the economy billions of pounds a year.

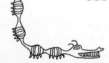

Furthermore, most civil liberties remain unused – when did a British citizen last express his or her right to demand a free packet of pork scratchings in a public house in return for shooting a troublesome rodent with a crossbow, as enshrined in the Magna Carta?[41] The standard British adult utilises on average between eight and twelve civil liberties per day, out of the possible 63,000 which have accumulated since the publication of the original Charter of Liberties in 1100. It is not unreasonable to suggest that all of these civil liberties could simply be consolidated into ten easily rememberable freedoms, to be used regularly and treasured.

- Small-talk to be outlawed in the workplace. The average office worker spends around 45 minutes a day indulging in small-talk. Cumulatively, pointless general chatter also costs the economy billions of pounds a year, money which could be ploughed back into schools, hospitals or skate parks.

- This small-talk prevention scheme would be simple to implement. Every employee would have to wear a badge detailing: how

---

41 The answer to this question is: in 1964, in The Leicester Arms, Penshurst, Kent.

they are;[42] how their partner and/or family is; whether or not they had a good evening/ weekend/holiday/operation; and who they currently think is best at being not that bad at skating/dancing/singing on the television. This simple, cheap and timesaving device would at a stroke remove 85% of the country's irrelevant conversations from the daily schedule.

- It would also increase the quality of our national discourse. If people knew their allowed conversation was limited, they would not waste so much of their interpersonal time on meaningless verbal jousting and low-probability flirting, and would instead embark instantly on a formal, structured discussion of the great political and philosophical issues of the age.

- Parliament to be replaced with a single computer wirelessly linked up to the brains of Britain's top four tabloid newspaper editors. This paperwork-saving plan would in effect merely be a streamlining of the current system.

- The armed forces to conduct their peace-keeping and occupation-based operations from

42 From a small range of regulation states of existence, **viz**: Great; Fine Thanks; So-So; and Not So Good.

Britain, via the internet. There is no reason in today's high-tech modern globalised global world why the military could not liaise with, cajole and coerce locals in Afghanistan and Iraq by means of regular blogs and podcasts concerning, for example: how to build a 20th-century-quality sewage system; the likely location of insurgent cells; roadblock etiquette; and the general joys of democracy.

- The armed forces to be privatised. It would make long-term economic sense for most nations to sell their armed forces to the private sector, and then lease them back as mercenary militia on the rare occasions when war actually breaks out. Thus the tax-payer would only foot the military bill at times when it is directly benefitting from it. The government would need to maintain only a medium-scale working nuclear arsenal, in case a country somewhere needs an emergency short-notice liberation.

- Lincolnshire to be sold. It is a traditional county with a good, traditional English heritage, but is of little strategic value to the modern UK. Most self-respecting Gulf-based billionaires would love to own a county as much as a football club. However any deal should contain certain basic safeguards to prevent any resumption of the pogroms into which medieval Lincoln occasionally lapsed.

Some of these measures may seem extreme, but the government's controversial bank bailouts have proved that these are extreme times, which call for interventionist measures. If the government is serious about saving the economy, and with it the entire nation (and it remains a medium-sized 'if'), it must have the courage to interfere in our daily lives with the same speculative abandon with which it has been poking the banking sector.

Isn't there an easier way of trimming a couple of noughts off the government annual spending spree?

Qassim al Zedatak, 42, freelance leg spinner, Karachi

Yes, but it would be controversial. Much of the current economicocrisis can be attributed to governments putting off tough decisions. Now, the nettle must not only be grasped, it must be eaten whole in one mouthful. And according to that nettle, the most effective way instantly to save billions of pounds for the exchequer would be to institute a maximum age limit of 80.

The elder part of the elderly part of the population is a great burden on the state – pensions and healthcare for the 80-plus necessarily rise as they cling with increasingly arthritic fingers to the crumbling precipice of existence. Few generate any taxable income beyond the occasional sale of a home-knitted tank top at a jumble sale (usually concealed from the taxman either by wily accountancy or dementia).

While state-run compulsory suicides for octogenarians might not, at first glance, be a vote-winner, this policy would without question prove to be surprisingly popular, as the cost savings generated would enable the government to propose an attractive, deal to its citizens. If people were to be guaranteed a good pension and high-quality free healthcare up to the age of 80, on the strict condition that on their 80th birthday they kill themselves, few people would quibble. In fact, a recent survey shows that 99% of people under the age of 79 would sign up for it immediately.

This scheme is clearly in the best economic interests of the country, and as such, in the current climate, it is in the best overall interests of the country too. It has the added practical bonus that the elderly can take control of their own deaths and choose exactly the manner of their own departure, rather than relying on the icy tentacles of fate to dole out their rough and painful justice. Succumbing in elongated agony to the mental and physical annihilation of geriatric decrepitude is no-one's idea of fun. Surely it would be far better to somersault off this mortal coil in a blaze of stage-managed glory – paragliding into an erupting volcano, being catapulted into a lunar orbit by Donny Osmond, driving a Lamborghini off the White Cliffs Of Dover whilst a novelty musical car horn honks the tune of 'We'll Meet Again', or teaming up with a twin sibling to jump into a lion enclosure dressed as a pantomime zebra.

Furthermore, just as Adam Hart-Davis and Moira Stewart have proven only too willing to act as government agents by desporting their love of taxation on national television, so there are a number of octogenarian celebrities who would be queuing up to set a heroic, historic example of self-sacrifice. Patriots such as Bruce Forsyth, Val Doonican, the Queen and the Duke of Edinburgh, Margaret Thatcher and Rolling Stone Keith Richards would literally jump at the chance, and would be seen off with varying degrees of enthusiasm by the public.

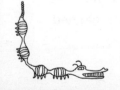

Neither I nor my friends are particularly enamoured of the idea of Financial Armageddon. What are your top six tips for surviving the Credit Crunch financially and psychologically intact?

Stan Francisco, 41, variety act, Los Angeles

1. Keep things in perspective. The Black Death was worse. You might have tough times ahead, but at least you can sneeze without having to cancel all of next week's appointments.

2. If a strange man approaches you and offers you some debt, politely turn him down. Then walk briskly away and call 999.

3. Formulate a revolutionary planet-changing invention, like the internet, television, or sliced bread. This should provide you with enough extra money to keep afloat.

4. Ignore it. Like a spoilt child, the Credit Crunch has behaved worse the more attention people and the media have paid it.

5. Kidnap the head of a major bank. Hold him hostage for a couple of months, then release him unharmed. The ensuing jail sentence will provide you with security and stability through these turbulent times. By the time you are released, any money you could have earned in the interim will probably be worthless anyway.

6. Make sure you were incredibly rich before the crisis started.

No offence, but none of those really appeal to me. Is there anything I can do to make everyday life cheaper?

Roquette Tristram-Lovejoy, 20, ink smuggler, Penzance

FIRSTLY, REDUCE YOUR OUTGOINGS on food. There are a number of ways you can achieve this.

Brace yourself to rummage through landfill sites for unopened tins and graze on the grass in public parks. For years, you've been putting off learning how to differentiate between poisonous berries and aniseed balls. Now is the time to do it.

Be prepared to try new foods. A slow-roasted fox is surprisingly edible if camouflaged with an extremely aggressive curry sauce (but make sure your butcher gives you fresh fox, preferably from a main road which you can trust).

It is also a little-known fact that if you dream about food, your stomach digests breakfast at three times its normal efficiency. If you draw your favourite snacks in marker pen on your pillowcase before bedtime every day, you will able

to reduce your morning bacon bap expenditure by 66.6%.

A creative way to cut down your food costs is to become an astronaut. Although in itself astronautcy does not pay particularly well – average NASA pro spacemen and spaceladies earn only £14,000 a year, and have to pay for their own helmets, as well as take-off and (usually) landing fees at Cape Canaveral. However, as an astronaut, not only will you not have to pay for meals whilst in space,[43] you will be a social curiosity and conversational certainty, and are therefore likely to be invited to at least three dinner parties a week. If you are prepared to let your dignity slide long enough to request a doggy bag at the end of your meal, your food expenditure can be reduced almost to zero.

Alternatively, and more achievably, simply **pretend** to be an astronaut. Make sure you have some authentic-looking photographs, a large selection of anecdotes about zero-gravity urination, and use the phrase "When you've seen the world

---

43 It is not possible to eat in zero gravity. Soviet cosmopooch Laika, the first doggie in space, died due to exhaustion caused by chasing a floating sausage around her cockpit. The early Apollo missions were dogged by problems of chicken nuggets which escaped at the first in-flight meal interfering with equipment for the rest of the voyage. NASA, believing that formal sit-down meals were essential for team bonding, simply banned all food once its rockets after blast-off.

from where I've seen the world..." at least once every thirty minutes.

Secondly, you should also slash your energy expenditure. There are a number of tried-and-tested means of doing this – knitting a giant poncho for your house to reduce your heating bill, investing in military-calibre night-vision goggles to lower your electricity usage, and saving on your water bill by covering yourself head to toe in soap before going jogging naked on a rainy day.

However, the best way to do minimise energy wastage is by hibernating. All economic winters come to an end eventually. In the meantime, hunker down with your family in a warm, dark place, surrounded by bedding made of shredded banknotes, and zonk out for a few years, or at least until Alistair Darling's eyebrows have come back down his head from their current petrified location near his hairline.

Will the Credit Crunch ruin Christmas?

> Natasha Kwan, 26, infant joy analyst,
> Bournemouth.

P OSSIBLY. MOST CHILDREN'S FIRST contact with the workings of economics is judging the

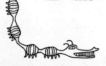

emotional worth of family members based on the financial value of the presents they give. If the economic troubles reduce Christmas gift expenditure, there could be a lot of stroppy children not wanting to play their new but obviously charity-shop-bought snakes and ladders game with a cash-strapped auntie.

If there is one thing that modern professional sport teaches us, other than the inherent unfairness of unbridled capitalism, it is that in any defeat, no matter how humiliating, 'positives' can be taken. If a football manager were talking to the media about the recent disastrous economic events, what obviously spurious positives would he pretend to take away to build on for next week's crucial crisis meeting, away from home at the World Bank?

Mahmoud Ahmadinejad, 52, Iranian president, Tehran

THIS ANSWER WAS KINDLY PROVIDED BY WILLIAM 'BLACKIE' GRAY, FORMER MANAGER OF 11-TIME FA CUP WINNERS MELCHESTER ROVERS:

WELL OBVIOUSLY THE CREDIT Crunch has beaten us and deservedly so, it caught us out on the day and maybe we weren't properly focused on the crisis after a difficult few months economically speaking. We made some basic errors out there, a couple of little lapses in concentration that cost us dear at the end of the day. We let the markets get right on top of us from the off, and all credit to them, but we know what we've done wrong and it's up to us to go out there and put it right next time.

But there are a lot of positives we can take away from this. We're a young economy, so we've got to go through these little ups and downs to pick up experience. We've learnt how important it is to keep our fiscal discipline under pressure. We've learnt that we can't afford to allow ourselves to be outmuscled in the middle of the park by the opposition speculators, or leave our defence exposed when the banks fail to track back.

Plus we've showed that we're prepared to put our money in our pockets to improve the economy when necessary, even if the fans don't always approve of what we're spending it on.

As they say, you're only as good as your handling of your last economic downturn, so we just need to put this crisis behind us, get back out there in the markets and do what we do best – capitalism.

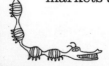

There are never any easy recessions in international economics these days, but in a way it's good for us that it has come around so quickly so we've got a chance to get straight back out there on the finance markets and put things right. And I'm confident that when the next crisis comes – and it will inevitably come at this level of finance – we'll be ready for it.

We've been working on our core economics skills in training – close control on the interest rates, getting tight on inflation, knowing when to play it short-term and when to knock it long-term. And you know maybe we need to be a little more defensively-minded when it comes to regulation. It might not be the most exciting form of economics, but you're judged on results at the end of the day, and whilst we work our way back up the table, we might need to rein things in a bit.

Or course I'm disappointed, we all are – there are a lot of economists who are hurting in that dressing room, let me tell you. I just hope the tax-payers and the chairmen are patient with us and get behind us, and I'm sure we'll come good when it matters. And look, it's not about me, it's about the economy, we're all in this together, it's a team effort and we win together, we lose together. OK, thanks Garth."

World economics has always seemed quite unfair to me. During the forthcoming financial nuclear winter resulting from the fallout from the Credit Crunch's 100 megaton monetary bomb, should we take the opportunity to try to create a more equal system for the planet?

Peach Blintz, 34, personal undersecretary, Miami

T HAT IS A SWEET idea. Unfortunately, it is one that will have to swim against a tide carrying thousands of years of economic history, with a large shipwreck of vested interests bobbing around on top.

In recent decades, the global economic system seems to have been based on an updated version of the ancient Chinese proverb: "Give a man a fish, and you will feed him for a day. But lease him a fishing rod, and you will feed yourself cut-price fish for a lifetime. Hey, that's a competitively cheap labour market you've set up right there, so well done; plus, since you own the rod, he had better fish, and fish bloody hard, otherwise no rod, and no rod means no wages, and no wages means no imported tinned fish, which is all he can now afford to buy to feed his family."

It has all been geared towards the realisation

of the Capitalist's ultimate dream: the illusion of competition with the guarantee of dominance.

The extent to which change can be achieved is reliant in large part on the efforts of individuals, as demonstrated by issues such as fair trade and the environment. Of course, change takes time, and without considerable assistance from governments and industry, the humble individual can feel like he or she is merely urinating into a slowly exploding volcano. Yes, it might make you feel better yourself – any wazz does – but it does not feel like you are really helping prevent the eruption.

However, the power of the collective consumer is a potent beast. This has been potently revealed by the multi-million-pound mobile phone ringtone industry. Twenty years ago, there was no demand for mobile phone ringtones. But consumers bravely demanded those ringtones, and, sure enough, they got those ringtones.

The increasing demand for fair trade and green products further illustrates this phenomenon. Unfair trade goods may be cheaper, but more and more people are wanting to eat their lunch without the faint whiff of human rights abuse clouding their nostrils. And many customers now like to drive cars that don't indirectly kill endangered ducks or drown our hypothetical grandchildren.

Businesses have reacted accordingly to satisfy their customers' shifting priorities, but they could do more. Supermarkets, for example, are already half-arsedly pricking our consumer conscience on behalf of the environment by charging for plastic bags; it would help the world considerably if our biggest food retailers took a similar step to support fair trade and discourage food wastage by staffing their checkouts with starving Third World children, who could flip us a bony-fingered bird and tell us where to stick ourselves whenever we are suckered into buying 18 ready-basted ostriches for the price of 17.

Most people like to have somewhere to live. That's a given. And it is nice to be able to put up your favourite Guns'n'Roses posters without worrying about your landlady throwing a saucepan at your head and screaming about the destructive powers of Blu-Tack. But why do people need to buy and own their houses?

Norbert 'Dentures' Sangel, 90, haulage specialist,
no fixed abode

THIS IS A RELATIVELY recent development. The attitude towards home ownership in medieval times could be summed up as: why buy a house when your life expectancy is 24? But times and aspirations have changed – people now set their sights a little higher than merely not dying of plague.

The desire to leap onto the property ladder intensified during the Margaret Thatcher years. The Grantham Granny was a divisive figure who did not merely split national opinion, she sliced it down the middle, sprayed whipped cream all over it and whacked a glacé cherry on top.

It became viewed as abnormal not to want to be mortgaged to and thus owned by a bank. People were bombarded with advertising slogans such as "Don't own your own house? L-l-loser", "Rent is bent", and "Why give all your money to a landlord when you could be giving it to a bank instead? And remember, there are millions of landlords, but there are only a few major banks still left in their natural high street habitat. They need your support."

However, with the current fall (or, in estate agent terminology, 'down-rise') in house prices, the property ladder has transpired to be one of those trick ladders used by circus clowns in window-cleaning sketches.

The government is rumoured to be reassessing its housing policy, and, as an alternative to home ownership, it will encourage young would-be first time buyers to live in a tent and put £100 on a randomly selected horse every Saturday.

My dead grandmother used to say to me, while she was still alive: "Learn your lessons, my boy/girl [delete as applicable], or I will fill your sleeping bag with centipedes again." Those lessons were: don't go camping with granny, and don't give granny a box of centipedes for her birthday. What lesson, or, preferably, lessons, could the world learn from the Credit Crunch?

Morislav Minovic, 70, duck egg magnate, Prague

THE PATH OF HISTORY is littered with the burnt-out remnants of lessons not learnt, as demonstrated by, for example, almost every story in almost every newspaper.

Hopefully, however, lessons will be learnt from the Credit Crunch. The first lesson is the importance of learning lessons (see Appendix 1). If these lessons had been learnt, we would not now need to learn them again.[44] The warnings were there, so witnessing irresponsible finance landing the world in another not particularly fine mess is like meeting a man who has lost both

---

44 One recently-imploded hedge fund actively prevented its staff from studying past mistakes and learning from history, and made them chant the company motto every morning before breakfast: "If you're learning, you're not earning."

hands in separate threshing machine accidents. To lose one hand in a threshing machine accident could reasonably be ascribed to misfortune or inexperience, perhaps even curiosity, or, at a stretch, horseplay. To lose both looks like he wanted to hurt himself.

The second lesson, as taught to the world by the sub-prime shenanigans,[45] is that if you lend large amounts of money to people who have absolutely no way of paying that money back, then they might not pay that money back.

This may seem obvious to the layman, but it could only be conclusively proved, beyond both reasonable and unreasonable doubt, by the age-old technique of trial and error.

Indeed, the advance of human civilisation has been a poorly-maintained rollercoaster of trials and errors. For example, cavemen only discovered through the pain of practical experimentation that putting their heads into the mouths of Tyrannosaurus Reges could result in serious injury to the face and neck. They had absolutely no way of knowing in advance that the big roaring dinosaurs had sharp teeth and healthy appetites. Only by risking failure could that crucial knowledge be acquired. This same process has

---

45 This has now been confirmed as the official classification, as adjudged by the World Bank's Folly Description Unit.

recurred in the sub-prime sector. We will all know better in future.

Other useful lessons that the world should consider learning in light of recent events include:

- Trade has become much more complicated since the old days of "an eye for an eye, a tooth for a tooth" transactions.[46]
- The whole of human commerce is based on the ability of some people to fool other people, and the willingness of those others to fool themselves.
- Leaving the markets alone without adequate supervision or regulation was like giving a child a giant tub of ice cream, telling it not to eat it, and nipping to the pub to watch the snooker for a few hours. If you are disappointed on your return to find an empty tub and a sticky child, you are a certifiable fool.

---

46 These encountered their first difficulties when they developed into the more complex "an eye now for two eyes in a year's time, and two teeth for a finger, now do we have a deal?" (Leviticus 28:13).

Inflation sky-rocketed to a stratospheric five per cent in 2008. Are we all doomed?

Michelle Dessler, 35, anti-terrorist officer,
Los Angeles

NOT YET. IT IS worth bearing in mind that other countries have even worse inflation than Britain: Zimbabwe, for example, which in July 2008 clocked up an impressive 231 million per cent annual inflation rate, and some claimed that even this was a conservative estimate. It would certainly be interesting to see the Bank Of England's Monetary Policy Committee try to quarter-point-interest-rate-tweak their way out of that kind of mess. If Zimbabwe can maintain this inflation rate for the next two years, then a penny fruit chew sent to a friend in Harare for Christmas 2008 will be worth £533 trillion by Christmas 2010. If you agree to split the profits 50/50 with your friend, you will both become the richest person in the world.

Throughout history, inflation has been hugely entertaining for neutral spectators of the currency markets. In 1946, it prompted the launch of the highest denomination banknote in history – the 100 quintillion pengő note, issued when Hungary went nought crazy after the end of the Second

World War. The historic bill featured the number 1 followed by twenty zeroes. The Soviet army later forced the locals to use more decimal points or face summary execution.[47]

---

47 Other significant notes from history include:

- The 204 million rouble note, issued by Peter The Great in 1711 to celebrate winning The Tallest Man in Russia competition for the fifth year in a row. Each million roubles represented a centimetre of Peter's winning height. Only one of these notes was ever printed, and the massive Tsar paid it to himself in prize money.

- The 500 billion lire note. The lire long held place as Europe's best-loved comic currency. It is rumoured that a suitcase-full of these rare notes sank to the bottom of Lake Como in 1938 when Benito Mussolini capsized his pedalo whilst trying to impress racing driver Alberto Ascari's girlfriend.

- The 1 trillion Ugandan shilling note, ordered specially by Idi Amin in the mid 1970s so he could make the world's richest origami pigeon.

In January 2009, Barack Obama will move into his plush new Washington house, be given the keys to Air Force 1, and take control of the most bulging in-tray in US presidential history. But what will he have to do to improve on the economic performance of his predecessor, George W. Bush?

Joe Biden, 66, future vice president
of the United States, Delaware

Nothing. He could literally do nothing and things would probably improve a bit. However, Obama thankfully seems to have higher ambitions than this, and the world is now looking to him for guidance on how best to clean up its economic vomit. As Shakespeare himself wrote: "In times of crisis, the world needs heroes."[48]

One significant factor in Obama's favour is the fact that he is replacing one of America's least popular presidents.[49] Bush will shuffle out of the back door of the White House then await the judgement of history like an Olympic figure skater sitting next to his silently fuming coach, looking

---

48 Hamlet Redux – The Director's Cut, Act 2 Scene 2.

49 Recent market research showed that, of the 3,421,901 limited-edition commemorative cuddly George Bush dolls sold since 2001 in America, more than 3 million now have needles jammed in them.

up at the judges' scoreboard with a grimace of concern, and hoping they don't mark him down too much for falling over five times in his routine, flipping a V-sign at them, and landing an unnecessary quadruple Salchow in the front row of the crowd, badly injuring a child.

Obama, for his part, can immediately set to work on chiselling his own face onto Mount Rushmore – because merely by virtue of following Bush into the Oval Office, he will seem to have been one of the five greatest presidents in American history. Following Bush into the White House is the political equivalent of following Mozart in a triple jump competition – no matter how bad you are, he has been dead since the 18th century. The watching world will be delighted just to see someone land in the sand-pit.

In mitigation, it must be said that Bush was one of America's unluckiest presidents. Having come to the Presidency through no real fault of his own in 2000, he had little opportunity to prepare himself for the rigours of running a multitrillion dollar business like the US. He was also hindered for some time by the Republican party's innate scepticism about the overall economic benefits of saving the world. And with the Iraq war, all he really did wrong was make a mistake at work – as we all have done at some point in our working lives. Bush was merely unfortunate to have had a job as the world's most powerful man when he made his workplace blooper.

Obama must also tackle the crisis head on, as in times of difficulty politicians tend to pass the buck like an especially exuberant Fijian sevens rugby team.[50] As the banking collapses unfolded like a bad soap opera, Bush accused Wall Street of having "got drunk". Perhaps for once the Texan Terrier deserves to be taken at face value – drunkenness is in fact the most logical explanation. How else could so many certified financial geniuses have conspired to make such a Jeroboam of Horlicks of the world economy through their harebrained short-termism and daredevil risk-taking? Alcohol must have generated excessive feelings of love towards their best friend, money, and they speculated with a boldness achievable only through booze-addled insensibility.[51] The entire crisis only

---

50 Few have held their hands up during the Credit Crunch and admitted culpability. It is rumoured that, during a Federal Reserve Class of '87 reunion at an adventure playground in Massachusetts in Autumn 2008, someone teased Alan Greenspan that the crisis was partly his fault. Greenspan burst into tears, shrieked, "You don't understand me, no-one understands me," and ran away across a field.

51 According to a recent Cambridge University report, another critical contributing factor in economic recklessness is testosterone. Overexcited traders apparently become so overwhelmed by their own unstoppable balls that they try to economically hump any share that moves, and the market

138

makes proper sense if Wall Street was indeed properly, continually, hammered. Admittedly, many argue that Wall Street was being plied with cheap Liebfraumilch by the Bush administration in an effort get it into bed, but the point stands.

Obama will have to confront a number of domestic and global issues to put the economy back on either the straight or the narrow, or, preferably, both. He will have to deal with the fact that a large part of the world's economically crucial oil reserves remains in the control of some of the world's jauntier leaders. He will have to try to persuade the bailed-out banks to try really hard not to balls up quite so hard next time. He will have to defuse the pensions time-bomb facing America.[52] He may have to moderate the excesses of Free Market economics.[53] He must take steps to ensure the economy is better prepared to withstand

---

crashes. So Obama might consider instituting a women-and-eunuchs-only policy for America's leading stock markets.

52 This is a problem facing all countries. There were also rumours on the Foreign Office fansite that North Korea has also developed a pensions time-bomb, which it has been parading around the streets of Pyongyang, and that the French have been testing their pensions time-bomb for several decades now, as a result of which there are now atolls in the South Pacific populated by nothing but grannies.

53 Under the Republicans, primary school children have been taught that whenever someone says they don't believe in free market economics, somewhere in the world an investment bank dies.

future 'glitches',[54] and to this end he must try to house-train the record-breaking Bush-era budget deficit before it permanent spoils America's economic carpet.

The crisis also presents opportunities for the new president. Many countries around the world are on the verge of bankruptcy. This gives Obama the chance to pick up some real bargains. Iceland, for example, could probably be bought for around $200,000, and become America's first new state since Hawai'i in 1959. This would make the USA technically part of Europe (again), giving it greater influence with the French, Germans, Andorrans and UEFA.

Overall, these are long-term problems which require long-term solutions, so perhaps the best thing Obama could do is to change the US constitution to give himself the 50-year term of office that would allow him the time to sort out the problem properly and sustainably. At least the majority of the world will be able to watch his attempts to deal with America's and the world's problems without wanting to throw a brick through their television screen – bad news for the global TV screen repair industry, which has enjoyed eight years of unprecedented boom.

---

54 Obama has already shown an ability to learn lessons from his mistakes. For example, after hurting his fingers in his car door, he now takes the precaution of putting on metal armoured gloves before he slams the car door on his hand.

And one final question. What is the solution to this whole sorry mess?

Robert B. Zoellick, 55, President, World Bank

D<small>ON'T KNOW. SORRY.</small>

THE END

APPENDIX 1: Could The Crisis Have Been Foreseen?

A LAN GREENSPAN, THE FORMER Chairman of the Federal Reserve and self-confessed big fan of sub-prime mortgages, told Congress in October 2008 that "We are in the midst of a once-in-a-century credit tsunami."

He said: "If all those extraordinarily capable people were unable to foresee the development of this critical problem, which undoubtedly was the cause of the world problem with respect to mortgage-backed securities, I think we have to ask ourselves: why is that? And the answer is that we're not smart enough as people. We just cannot see events that far in advance. And unless we can, it's very difficult to look back and say, 'Why didn't we catch something?'"

That is Greenspan's view, and he is one of those extraordinarily capable people.

Here are some further words of wisdom from other extraordinarily capable people who by contrast did foresee various problems ahead. Please note the dates when they did their foreseeing.

"We try to be alert to any sort of mega-catastrophe risk, and that posture may make us unduly appreciative about the burgeoning quantities of

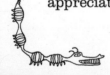

long-term derivatives contracts and the massive amount of uncollateralized receivables that are growing alongside. In our view, however, derivatives are financial weapons of mass destruction, carrying dangers that, while now latent, are potentially lethal."

Warren E. Buffett, legendary billionaire business whizz, 2002[55]

"If all the bank loans were paid, no one could have a bank deposit, and there would not be a dollar of coin or currency in circulation. This is a staggering thought. We are completely dependent on the commercial Banks. Someone has to borrow every dollar we have in circulation, cash or credit. If the Banks create ample synthetic money we are prosperous; if not, we starve. We are absolutely without a permanent money system. When one gets a complete grasp of the picture, the tragic absurdity of our hopeless position is almost incredible, but there it is. It is the most important subject intelligent persons can investigate and

55 Buffett, one of the world's richest men and therefore someone who clearly knows, in business terms, that it is better to hold the toasting fork than the marshmallow, has also said: "In the business world, the rear-view mirrow is always clearer than the windshield." It appears that Greenspan's rear-view mirror may have had one of those dangly air-freenshers hanging in front of it, in the shape of dollar sign.

reflect upon. It is so important that our present civilization may collapse unless it becomes widely understood and the defects remedied very soon."

Robert H Hemphill, credit manager of Federal Reserve Bank of Atlanta, 1934

"The Government should create, issue, and circulate all the currency and credits needed to satisfy the spending power of the Government and the buying power of consumers. By the adoption of these principles, the taxpayers will be saved immense sums of interest. Money will cease to be master and become the servant of humanity."

Abraham Lincoln, professional President and three-time Hat Wearer of the Year, 1865

"I see in the near future a crisis approaching that unnerves me and causes me to tremble for the safety of my country; corporations have been enthroned, an era of corruption in High Places will follow, and the Money Power of the Country will endeavor to prolong its reign by working upon the prejudices of the People, until the wealth is aggregated in a few hands, and the Republic is destroyed. I feel at this moment more anxiety for the safety of my country than ever before, even in the midst of war."

Abraham Lincoln, professional President and two-time Hat Wearer of the Year, 1864

"It is said that the world is in a state of bankruptcy, that the world owes the world more than the world can pay."

**Ralph Waldo Emerson, philosopher
and essayist, 18??**

"I believe that banking institutions are more dangerous to our liberties than standing armies. If the American people ever allow private banks to control the issue of their currency, first by inflation, then by deflation, the banks and corporations that will grow up around them will deprive the people of all property until their children wake up homeless on the continent their fathers conquered."

**Thomas Jefferson, freelance founding father,
Declaration of Independence writer
and President, 1802**

"The national budget must be balanced. The public debt must be reduced; the arrogance of the authorities must be moderated and controlled. Payments to foreign governments must be reduced, if the nation doesn't want to go bankrupt."

**Cicero, Roman statesman, lawyer,
general know-all, 55BC.**

APPENDIX 2:
Bank Of England Facts

- The Bank Of England is known affectionately as 'The Old Lady'. This is due to its excessive caution with money, vulnerability to obvious scams, concern that its fellow central banks around the world keep dying off, refusal to trust any youngsters who knock on its front door, inability to keep up with global trends, and the facts that people panic whenever it looks like collapsing, and are more interested in its money than anything it has to say.

- Not since 1993 has the Bank Of England had a governor who has not shared the surname or full name of a two-time runner-up in the World Darts Championship. From 1993, Bank chief Eddie George was the proud co-holder of an identical surname as the legendary candlestick-wielding 1980 and 1994 losing finalist Bobby George; Eddie's successor Mervyn King took this scheme one step further by being the 100% namesake of Mervyn King, runner-up at Frimley Green in 2002 and 2004. It is not known how the economy would be affected by a Bank Of England governor without a darts-related name. And may the Lord save us from ever having to find out.

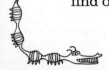

- The Bank Of England was, ironically, founded by, of all people, a Scotsman – William Paterson, in 1694. Only time will tell whether it will also be bankrupted by a Scotsman.

- If inflation misses the government's target rate by more than 1%, the Governor has to write a letter to the Chancellor of the Exchequer explaining what the hell has gone wrong. If it misses by less than 1%, but more than 0.5%, the Governor must send the Chancellor a postcard marked 'sorry'. And if the inflation bullseye is missed by more than 2%, the Governor has to send the Chancellor a box of chocolates, one of those novelty greetings cards that plays a tune when opened, and some slinky underwear to make him feel better.

APPENDIX 3:
Things That Have Been Thought Too Big To Fail, But Which Have, Nonetheless, Failed

Bruhathkayosaurus

Claim To Fame: World's Largest Ever Dinosaur.

Estimated weight: 200,000 kilograms (approx. 1 million kebabs).

Current Status: Extinct. Totally extinct.

Point Of Weakness: Vulnerability to sudden asteroid strike.

Verdict: Big, but Failed.

Woolly Mammoth

Claim To Fame: Largest Ever Elephant.

Maximum Tusk Length: 3.5 metres (approx. 14 kebab sticks).

Current Status: Extinct. Perhaps not as extinct as the Bruhathkayosaurus, but still as extinct as anyone could wish to be.

Point Of Weakness: Ice Age – not woolly enough.

Verdict: Big, but Failed.

Roman Empire

Claim To Fame: Co-founder of European Civilisation, original developer of reality entertainment, European Road Building Champions for 324 consecutive years.

Largest recorded bigness: Controlled 2.3 million square miles of prime real estate, stretching from Newcastle to Jerusalem (both cities which claim to be homes of Messiahs) and beyond.

Current Status: Vatican City – 0.17 square miles. Used to be more than 13 million times bigger than it is now.

Point Of Weakness: Nutty emperors, lead poisoning, obsession with feeding people to lions, tendency to goad Visigoths, rude mosaics, orgies.

Verdict: Big, but Ultimately Failed.

HMS Titanic

Claim To Fame: Massive ship, massive fun.

Maximum capacity: 3,500 people, anything up to 2 lifeboats.

Current Status: Wet.

Point Of Weakness: Allergy to Ice, Cocky Assumptions Of Unsinkability.

Verdict: Big, succeeded in short-term, but, in the long run, Failed.

Washington Mutual

Claim To Fame: USA's 6th largest bank, largest savings and loan association.

Assets Held in 2007: $327 billion.

Current Status: Bankrupt.

Point Of Weakness: Greed-idiocy combination endemic in global economics.

Verdict: Big, but Failed.

Epitaph: Oooops.

APPENDIX 4: Glossary of 10 Important Financial Terms

Boom & Bust: The natural reproductive cycle of the economy. The boom is so called because it is like a nuclear bomb test – great fun for everyone at the time, but causing long-term problems that no-one fully comprehends or cares about at the time. The bust is so called because the people who caused it end up looking like tits.

Bear Market: A market in which share prices are falling and confidence is low. Named after the famous woodland-soiling mammal, the bear, because it can be easily tranquilised, chained up, and taught to dance by ruthless speculators.

Bull Market: A market in which share prices are rising and confidence is high. Named after farm animal and Spanish sports star, the bull. The 'bull market' is so called because, like the bull, it is stupid, and never plans for its long-term future.

Credit Crunch: A big-time shortage of credit and money. Occurs when banks realise that they don't know what they're doing, why they're doing it, or how they're going to pay for it if they do it. Results in higher mortgage and loan costs for consumers,

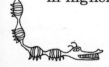

many of whom were tricked into borrowing with advertising slogans such as "Come on, it's basically free money", "14.9% APR – that works out at about £5 a year I think", and "F*** the future".

Derivatives: Financial instruments which don't exist. Rather than buying and selling a commodity itself, derivatives traders will essentially gamble with each other on issues related to it. For example, rather than purchasing a blouse, derivatives traders place bets on the number of admiring looks the blouse will get at a dinner party, whether the blouse will be worn more than once, and whether it will shrink in the wash.

Derivatives trading is a risky business due to the inherently unreliable nature of things that don't actually exist, but don't worry, the worldwide market for derivatives is only worth around $1,000 trillion, or, if you want to use a number that doesn't get much air time, $1 quadrillion. That is around 15 times the entire planet's GDP. Fingers crossed.

Hedging: 1. Covering your financial back.

                2. An illicit sexual practice in which fat cat business people meet in the middle of the night in the undergrowth outside a motorway service station and arouse each other by revealing their annual bonus.

Recession: A period of economic decline often brought about by the prediction of a period of economic decline. To put it in context for those unfamiliar with recessions, they are not as bad as lethal worldwide cholera epidemics, but they are worse than your nation being knocked out of the World Cup. An economy in recession, were it to be admitted to a hospital, would be described by doctors as being 'in a serious but stable condition', although they might add that it is too early to speculate on whether any lasting damage has been done, or whether it will be able to function independently in the future.

Run on the banks: When bank customers withdraw their money from a bank after overhearing a guy in the pub or on the television say that bank customers have started withdrawing their money from the bank. Unifies the two great British hobbies of panicking and queuing. Not to be confused with the annual Running of the Banks at the San Mateo Apóstol festival in Pamplona, Spain, when herd of bank executives is let loose onto the streets of the city, and members of the public flee for their financial lives as the bankers try to skewer them on their punitive interest rates.

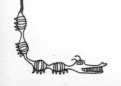

Stagflation: When inflation and stagnation finally get it together after years of staring at each other lustfully over the economic dance floor. They're obviously not suited to each other, their relationship upsets a lot of people, but they don't care. They're in love.

Sub-Prime Mortgage: A mortgage for the poor. Due to the borrower not having any money, there is an increased risk that they will not be able to pay the mortgage back, so the bank covers this risk by making the mortgage more expensive, increasing the increased risk that the borrower will not be able to pay the mortgage back. The number of borrowers not paying their mortgages back causes panic in the economic world, leading to interest rates rising, thus increasing the increased increased risk that borrowers will not be able to pay their mortgages back. As sensible as checking whether your gas oven is working properly by switching it on, sticking your head in it, and seeing if you're still alive two hours later.

Bibliography of suggested further reading

How To Make Money And Appal People
by Midas 'Guts' Sphogatis (1989)

The famously uncouth Greek billionaire shares the secrets that have made him one of the world's richest and most unpopular human beings. Sphogatis, once described by rival Aristotle Onassis as "an indefatigable arsehole", first made his money selling hot chilli sauce to kebab vans and gastric medicines to their customers.

The Great Depression – A Biography Of 1920s Wall Street's Most Prophetic Light Entertainer
by Scruton X. McLouth (1998)

McLouth, primarily an author of financial stories for children (<u>Hopalong Hedgehog's Happy Hedge Fund</u>, <u>Mr Minted and Percy Profit Margin Go Laughing All The Way To The Bank</u> and <u>Goldilocks And The Three Bear Markets</u>) details the extraordinary life of Mansforth Scrage, a.k.a. 'The Great Depression', who strutted the boards in the burlesque clubs and pool halls of early 20th century Wall Street, warning about impending economic catastrophe through the medium of provocative dancing and washboard music.

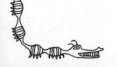

In Praise Of Corporation Tax – A Collection Of Poems
by the staff of PriceWaterhouseCoopers (2002)

Outstanding anthology of socially-responsible business verse from legendary accountancy firm. Winner of the 2003 Norman Lamont Memorial Silver Salver for financial poetry.

Karl Marx And The Aubergine
by C.S. Lewis (1948)

The man who put Narnia on the map also wrote a collection of short stories for teenagers about macroeconomics. Published to commemorate the 100th anniversary of Marx's smash hit bourgeois-bashing romp The Communist Manifesto, the title story tells of how a magic aubergine called Auberon tried to persuade little Karl that a classless society, although theoretically utopian, could never work in practice. The sequel, Karl Marx And The Moussaka, is considered Lewis's darkest work.

Dispensing the Indispensable IV – How To Sleep At Night, & Other Corporate Guilt-Reducing Advice
by Dr Millicent Strahan (2005)

American daytime TV's Millie Millions offers her latest handy everyday tips on everything from how to justify stratospheric bonuses, how to blithely ignore massive job cuts further down the economic food chain, and how to convince yourself that tax is voluntary.

101 Ways To Destroy A Bank
by Tony Hart

Hilarious cartoons about stock market manipulation by former TV art presenter Hart, now widely regarded as Britain's greatest ever painter.

Capitalism or Tennis?
by Warren Buffett & Mats Wilander (2001)

Billionaire investor and three-time French Open winner each put forward reasons why their chosen profession offers the best solutions for a sustainable economic future for the planet.

100 Greatest Stock Market Flotations
by Fahey, Woodward & Dallin (2008)

The three original members of 1980s girl pop supergroup Bananarama reconvene for their first joint project since 2002, to analyse their favourite companies' entries onto the London Stock Exchange.

Is Your Child Speculating On The Derivatives Market?
by Professor Geraldine Hoörskoch (2004)

Celebrity Dutch child psychiatricist gives invaluable advice for all concerned parents in the electronic age. It can be impossible to fully monitor your little ones' internet use, so Hoörskoch details the tell-tale signs that could highlight a secret problem – such as nervous or withdrawn behaviour, suddenly having millions of pounds in a Post Office savings account, or crying uncontrollably when the latest market figures are read out on the news.

Horace – My Story
by Horace (with W.E.Oddie)

Ghosted autobiography of Alan Greenspan's magic budgerigar, who for 19 years from 1987 to 2006 was considered the most significant pet in world economics. Fed-head Greenspan convinced the world to rely on his colourful parakeet's supernatural financial powers to make sure that the catastrophically indebted system would be fine. For years, the system worked, but when Horace refused to work for his owner's successor, Ben Bernanke, the flaws in Greenspanish economics became obvious. A frank, witty, no-holds-barred look at a fascinating life.

Suggested Hip-Hop Discography

Plu2Cratz - 'Hang Seng Horror'

Strutting, arrogant rant about problems in the Asia-Pacific markets from the vulture capitalist Harlem rapper.

Li'l Dividend feat. The Profit Prophet - 'Short-Sell Shirley (She Ain't Worth Nothing)'

Misogyny meets market opportunism in Dre-influenced collaboration between two of LA's smartest investor DJs. Produced by Lord (formerly Sir) Mixalot.

Wurkhas In Burkhas – 'No Interest (Sharia The Wealth)'

Communist Muslim girl group's paean to the benefits of both shared ownership and the in-built restraints of Islamic economics. Angry two-pronged blast at Western financial structures. Part Public Enemy, part public library.

Marky Marx and the Fund Bunch – 'Woops, There It Was'

Thumping bass lines and a cavalcade of obscenities from the former Specul8 front man and his new crew, as they relate how they lost $10 million on a single futures swap.

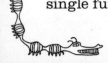